*Should I Medicate
My Child?*

ALSO BY LAWRENCE H. DILLER

Running on Ritalin

Should I Medicate My Child?

Sane Solutions for Troubled Kids With—and Without—Psychiatric Drugs

Lawrence H. Diller, M.D.

BASIC
BOOKS

A Member of the Perseus Books Group

Disclaimer

This book is designed to help you make informed choices; it is not meant to replace treatment by a physician or other licensed health care provider in the diagnosis or treatment of emotional or behavior problems in children.

Note: Many of the cases in this book are based on composites of families I have met in my professional experience. Where cases are based on individuals I have encountered in my medical practice, I have changed the names, sex, family constellations, and occupations to protect the subjects' privacy.

Copyright © 2002 by Lawrence H. Diller

Published by Basic Books,
A Member of the Perseus Books Group

All rights reserved. Printed in the United States of America. No part of this book may be reproduced in any manner whatsoever without written permission except in the case of brief quotations embodied in critical articles and reviews. For information, address Basic Books, 10 East 53rd Street, New York, NY 10022-5299.

Designed by *Brent Wilcox*

A cataloging-in-publication record for this book is available from the Library of Congress.
ISBN 0-465-01645-6

FIRST EDITION

02 03 04 / 10 9 8 7 6 5 4 3 2 1

For
DENISE, MARTIN,
and LOUIE

CONTENTS

ACKNOWLEDGMENTS

Writing a second book reminded me in some ways of purchasing a second house: The process was not quite as mystifying or frightening the second time around. Nevertheless, I benefited from the help and advice of many, whom I wish to acknowledge and thank.

Once again the openness and support of the families I treat astonished and delighted me. Their stories and words provide a richness of drama and detail I could never come up with on my own. Their willingness to assist others in distress is a tribute to their generosity and selflessness, often when they are in great pain themselves.

Since the publication of my first book, *Running on Ritalin*, many individuals have provided me with materials, ideas, and support. They include Jon Weil, Sabrina Morganti, Mary Jane Nunes-Temple, Sue Parry, Jack Obedzinski, William Carey, Gretchen LeFever, Julie Zito, Gretchen Feussner, Sam Goldstein, Peter Kramer, Erik Parens, Stanley Turecki, Peter Jensen, Anne Rees, and Thom Hartmann. Rich Simon of the *Psychotherapy Networker* and Karen Kroft and Jennifer McSweeney of Salon.com have all supported my ongoing writing by regularly publishing my work. Thanks also to the parent/reader/friends who reviewed the manuscript: Jennifer Chinlund, Linda Detert, Cecille Gunst, and Kathy Moody.

My early discussions on bipolar disorder with Phillip Rappaport of Free Press Books led directly to a book proposal on the broader subject of children's psychiatric medications. My former editor at Bantam Books, Toni Burbank, who introduced me to the person who helped so much in writing the manuscript, is the godmother of this book.

Special thanks go to Paul Wilson, vice president of IMS America, who has repeatedly provided me drug prescription data at no cost. His generosity and thoughtfulness about the issues are remarkable, especially within the industry context.

I am enormously indebted to Glen Elliott, chief of the Children's Division of the Langley-Porter Neuropsychiatric Institute of the University of California–San Francisco. For the second time Glen has provided the peer review for my books. His humility and humor belie an expertise and experience as a guide through the uncharted territories of psychiatric drug use in children for me and countless other professionals in the Bay area.

Members of my family once again supported and put up with the obsessional demands that go with writing a book. My sons, Martin and Louie, have grown up hearing their dad, either at the dinner table or on television, talk about serious matters. They understood at an early age the issues involved, and their comments demonstrate to me a wisdom and maturity that make me very proud. My wife, Denise, remains my rock and basic support. She provides a healthy moderating perspective on both my ideas and my ego. I continue to depend on her greatly. My sister, Vivian Diller, a psychologist, and her husband, John Jacobs, a psychiatrist, have consistently been there for me both intellectually and emotionally. I am lucky to have a wonderful mother-in-law, ex-special education teacher Lynda Bostrom, who read an early draft and provided insightful comments. My nonagenarian writer-author aunt, Sandra, is not only a big support but an unlikely continuing prod to my productivity. ("I hope you already have an idea for your third book, Larry.")

Jo Ann Miller, my editor at Basic Books, provided continuing support and wise counsel, not the least of which is based on her experiences with her own children and grandchildren. Beth Vesel, my agent, has been a steady companion and friend through two books and the raising of our own children. Her belief in me and my ideas is an inspiration.

I reserve my final and most enduring thanks to Leigh Ann Hirschman, a writer who worked at reshaping and polishing the structure and language of my initial manuscript. Leigh Ann's brilliant conceptions and crystal-clear rewriting have enormously contributed to the success of the final product. Her rigorous demands on herself and me were a perfect response to my sometimes flagging effort of nearly three years. I am delighted that she will shortly be learning, as I did, that the challenges and the rewards of raising one's own children are far greater than can be imagined.

PART ONE

Eight Questions to Ask Yourself
Before Accepting or Rejecting Medication

1

Weighing Your Options

Brandon has just turned three and is driving his parents crazy. He has temper tantrums several times daily, beating his arms, legs, and even his head against the floor. On one frightening occasion, he cut his temple on the corner of the fireplace mantel. When his parents try to hold him in their arms for protection, he kicks, bites, and hits them, arching his back until he wriggles out of their grasp.

Tantrums are not the only problem. Brandon picks up and tosses aside toys as if he were a human weed whacker; despite his mother's constant efforts to maintain control over her son's behavior, the house is strewn with plastic animals, toy race cars, and broken games. His parents are embarrassed to let Brandon play at anyone else's house, and they have noted the disapproving looks of visitors. They would like to teach Brandon to pick up his toys, but all attempts so far have only yielded more of his violent tantrums—which, his exhausted parents agree, they want to avoid whenever possible.

Carrie, Brandon's mother, dislikes the idea of giving psychiatric medications to children. She would prefer alternative therapies and has already consulted a food allergist. She is considering eliminating sugar from Brandon's diet. But, she tells me, no one else she knows has a child like this. She wonders aloud: If Brandon has a disorder that makes him hyper and unhappy, wouldn't it be cruel not to give him a drug that would help?

Eight-year-old Ruth cries every morning before she goes to school. "No one likes me," she says, adding that the teacher is mean. But the teacher has told Ruth's parents that their daughter is doing well in school, both academically and socially. When Ruth is introduced to new people, she won't talk and sometimes tries to crawl under her mother's coat.

But with her family, Ruth is a Mr. Hyde. She insists on wearing only T-shirts and blue jeans—and throws a fit if her mother insists that she wear something different, like, God forbid, a dress. In the midst of her tantrums, she's yelled, "You're horrible! I'm going to kill myself!"

Natalie, Ruth's mother, has tried techniques ranging from patience and reassurance to antianxiety medication for her daughter. But she feels it's only a matter of time before her family implodes under the pressure of the child's extreme sensitivity. "How do I know if she needs a different drug?" Natalie asks me, her voice constricting. "Or if I've just been a lousy parent?"

Jerry, nearly sixteen, came home with two Ds and two Fs on his latest report card. His parents recall a time when Jerry was an A student, but now he ignores major assignments as well as his homework. He doesn't appear to have a behavior problem, but it's hard to tell: Jerry spends most of his time these days in his room with the door closed, presumably on the computer or the telephone. Nor does he seem to lack for intellectual ability, since he still pulls a B+ in history—a subject he has always liked—and is enthralled by the cerebral computer game Myst.

A relative mentioned that many of Jerry's traits fit the profile for attention deficit/hyperactivity disorder, inattentive type. His mother, Joyce, is concerned that her son needs medical care. Rick, his father, thinks that Jerry is just plain lazy. But Joyce is quick to point out that Rick works a seven-day week, is often on the road, and doesn't have the opportunity to notice the subtleties of their son's behavior. For his part, Jerry agrees with his father's diagnosis of laziness. However, he has volunteered that he is willing to take medication. "But it can't have any bad side effects," he declares.

Although Anna and Steven MacAteer agree that their daughter Susie is "high energy," they do not report misbehavior from her at home. But the teacher at the private Christian school where Susie is a second grader has *been calling Anna nearly every week. Susie drifts away from her work, constantly getting out of her seat to visit the bathroom, chat with her friends, or play with the class aquarium. Punishments like missing recess or going to time-out seem to have no effect on her behavior. The teacher thinks that Susie should see a doctor for testing. The tone in her voice makes it clear the point behind the "suggestion": If Susie doesn't improve soon, she will be asked to leave the school.*

Anna and Steven do not want their daughter to receive a psychiatric label so early in her life, nor do they like the idea of giving her a drug to improve her behavior. But they aren't sure which is worse—medicating their child for a disorder they're not sure she has or risking expulsion from a school she enjoys.

This book is for parents of children like Brandon, Ruth, Jerry, and Susie, who, from toddlers to teens, are experiencing behavior or emotional problems. These problems range in kind and severity. The child may be angry, intense, distractible, energetic, strong-willed, obsessive, fearful, shy, listless, or remote; or she may have difficulty forming normal relationships with other people.

If you are a parent of such a child, you have probably sought out and received plenty of advice, none of it entirely successful and some of it disastrous. By the time parents arrive in my office, they have usually run through a series of approaches: time-outs, negotiation and compromise, reward systems, reassurance, and so on. The parents are worried, naturally, about their child's mental health and prospects for the future. Will she struggle with this problem throughout her life? Will it ultimately keep her from getting a good job or making a happy marriage? What will happen to her self-esteem? Often parents experience battle fatigue; it's common for them to feel guilty and confused or angry at the not-so-subtle sense of blame imposed on them by schools and other parents. They often feel tyrannized by their child's problems and long for escape. "I'd love to spend a week—no, a month—on a deserted island," one mother told me, the circles under her eyes like blue half-moons. These fantasies, which are perfectly normal, can be terribly distressing for parents, who may fear that they indicate a secret lack of commitment to their child.

Parents who have reached this point often come to me because they know that I am licensed to prescribe psychiatric drugs to children and have many years of experience doing so. On the first visit they usually ask, *Does my child need medication?*

There is no easy answer to that question. If you are reading this book, the prospect of giving psychiatric drugs to your child probably leaves you with mixed feelings. You may not be sure what these drugs do or how they help. You are probably worried about side effects. If your child is already taking medication, you may be asking yourself whether you've made the right choice—even if the drug appears to be helping. Like many parents I see, you may be uneasy with the number of prescriptions written for children these days and wonder if our culture sometimes uses medication to shoehorn children into a one-size-fits-all mold of smiling compliance.

You may also worry about the repercussions of *not* medicating your child. All of us involved in a child's treatment frequently worry that ongoing problems will cause the child to lose hope. "Why even try?" she might say in response to a challenging homework assignment or a situation that requires self-control. "I'm just a dumb/bad/weird kid." Like Natalie, the mother of Ruth, you may fear for the well-being of the rest of the family. Like Anna and Steven MacAteer, you may be weighing the act of medicating your child, thereby ensuring that she will stay in her current classroom, versus the threat of expulsion or placement in a special class.

Both sets of concerns are present in loving parents who want their child to be healthy and happy. I've written this book for parents who want to see how a thoughtful doctor—one who keeps these same concerns constantly in mind—thinks through the problem of psychiatric medication on a case-by-case basis. My hope is to help you make a difficult decision from a stance that is as informed and balanced as possible.

Battle of the B Movies

I am a behavioral pediatrician—a medical doctor (M.D.) with a specialty in children's behavioral and developmental problems—who has been practicing for more than twenty years in Walnut Creek, California, a suburb of San Francisco. I have evaluated and treated more than twenty-five hundred children with emotional, behavioral, and performance problems at home or at school. Trained in family therapy, I work with the parents and siblings of these children as well.

The skyrocketing rate of Ritalin use in the 1990s led me to write a book called *Running on Ritalin,* in which I addressed the bureaucratic, social, medical, and economic forces squeezing parents and doctors into rushing to treat kids' behavior problems with that drug. Since then, the use of other psychiatric drugs—antidepressants, antipsychotics, anticonvulsants, and so on—for children has exploded as well. I've appeared on many television and radio shows to discuss this phenomenon. When producers are screening me for these appearances, they often ask, Dr. Diller, are you for psychiatric drugs in children, or against them?

The question itself reflects the hyperbolic debate that has been waged on the airwaves for the last decade or so. Robert Fancher, reviewing *Running on Ritalin* for the *Washington Post,* likened the process to "dueling B movies," in which heroes and villains battle for the souls of children in an atmosphere of Gothic dimensions. In one of these hypothetical movies, doctors who prescribe medications are noble knights, their chargers aloft, freeing children and their families from the tyranny of a biologically based mental illness. In the other scenario, physicians—especially psychiatrists—are child-hating mad scientists who sedate and control our youth at the behest of their lazy parents and teachers. These dramatic scenarios appeal to television talk shows and tabloid journalism, but they don't do justice to people who are struggling with unhappy, difficult children.

In answer to that question—am I for or against psychiatric drugs for children—I say something like this: I'm certainly not against them. In the last year, I wrote more than four hundred prescriptions for Ritalin or its equivalent. I also prescribe, although much less frequently, antidepressants, major tranquilizers, and mood stabilizers. I'm "for" psychiatric drugs in the same way I'm "for" antibiotics. When antibiotics are used judiciously, they can save lives. But those who reach for antibiotics at every sniffle and cough, regardless of the underlying cause, endanger us all by encouraging strains of resistant bacteria. No drug, including psychiatric medication, is either good or bad. Drugs are simply tools that can be used with a greater or lesser degree of judgment.

But parents don't buy books titled "Should I Give My Child Penicillin?" Applying good judgment to an antibiotic is not as difficult: It attacks an identifiable agent of disease; its targets—bacteria—produce recognizable symptoms; and its side effects and contraindications are well-known. Not so for psychiatric drugs.

Psychiatric drugs do not target an invasive organism. Rather, they are directed toward the child's brain, the very center of personality and of the functions that define who we are. There are no clear tests, no X rays, no MRI scans, that tell us when a child should be labeled with a certain behavioral or emotional condition or receive psychoactive medication. Although we can hazard some good guesses about their efficacy, we do not know for sure if many of these drugs actually improve the problems for which they are prescribed. None of us—doctors, parents, researchers, pharmaceutical companies, lawmakers—knows for certain what kinds of long-term side effects these drugs might cause when given to children, with their still developing bodies and brains. If psychiatric drugs are tools, they do not come with a clear set of instructions. The best we can do is to think thoroughly through what we know—about the side effects, the benefits, and the dangers of withholding medication from a child in trouble—while constantly reminding ourselves of all that we do not know.

Who's Minding the Scales?

I feel strongly that the decision to medicate can be made only after the benefits of a specific medication for an individual child are carefully weighed against the potential risks. I also want to be sure that appropriate nondrug interventions have been tried. I have had excellent results with behavioral strategies that help kids avoid drugs or reduce their need for them.

To my mind, this approach is neither radical nor reactionary. It's simply the way a doctor is trained to handle any potent drug, especially one whose effects are not fully understood. It's a matter of basic medical ethics.

Yet I know the pressure on parents and doctors to medicate—quickly, as a first line of action when problems arise—is so intense that ethics are sometimes pushed out of the picture. The statistics tell a disturbing story. Approximately 5 million children in America take at least one psychiatric drug; the number of kids I see on two or three simultaneous medications grows exponentially with each passing year. According to IMS Health, the pharmaceutical industry's equivalent of the Nielsen ratings service, the use of Prozac-like drugs for children was up 74 percent between 1995 and 1999. During that same period, the use of mood stabilizers, not including lithium, rose by 4,000 percent, and prescriptions for new antipsychotic medications like Risperdal have grown by nearly 300 percent. According to DEA statistics, production of Ritalin increased by over *700 percent* between 1990 and 1998.

I see the real-life counterparts to these statistics walk into my office every day, kids like Doug, a five-year-old in constant motion whose developmental milestones appeared to be one to two years behind normal. His previous doctor tried several medications to calm him down but did not find the time to explore Doug's developmental problems and their impact on his parents' ability to manage him. I called the doctor to share my thoughts about Doug. "Sorry," he told me, in a resigned and apologetic voice, "but I have to see a kid every fifteen minutes. It's the only way I can make an income under managed care."

Or take Bobby, an impulsive, angry third grader who was on Dexedrine (a stimulant), Anafranil (originally used in adult depression and obsessive-compulsive disorder but here prescribed at night for its sedating effect), and Neurontin (an anticonvulsant). No one talked to his parents about how to set limits and enforce house rules effectively; the problem of his parents' brutal divorce was given barely a nod. It was assumed that Bobby's anger was rooted in a "chemical imbalance" that could be fixed by medication. When one drug didn't work, his doctors simply added yet another to the mix.

It's possible to argue that these statistics and my experience reflect an increasingly sophisticated and compassionate attitude toward mental illness in children. We finally recognize the biological nature of mental illness, this argument runs, and at last we have the appropriate treatment at our disposal. To an extent, I agree. Anyone who has seen a truly hyperactive child who is able to play with her friends thanks to Ritalin or Adderall would feel the same way.

But when I talk with families and professionals in the office, at dinner parties, and during conferences, I hear an echo of my own professional qualms. Most of us are uneasy with how quickly and how far the numbers have shot up. It doesn't take much imagination to put the statistics together with ever increasing classroom size, heavy burdens on parents at work, the relentless drumbeat of pharmaceutical advertising, and the pressure on doctors from HMOs to find treatments that require as little office time as possible. Add to that the little that is actually known about how these drugs act in children's bodies, and I think it's fair to ask: Are we forgetting to consider the risks of drugs as well as the benefits? Who is keeping an eye on the scales?

One popular reaction to the wave of prescriptions for kids is to dismiss psychoactive drugs altogether. But adherents of this philosophy ignore the fact that drugs can sometimes be very useful, especially when children are suffering so much that their schooling or safety is in jeopardy. A more sophisticated response to the statistics is to gather the information that will help you weigh all your options.

As a parent, you have the ultimate responsibility for medication. Doctors and psychiatrists can make recommendations, and your child can have some input, but in the end, *you* are the person who decides whether your kid takes a little yellow pill with breakfast. Given the current climate, in which psychoactive drugs seem to be dispensed as readily as Tylenol, you'll need to ask the hard questions, make the tough calls, and always keep a close watch on that scale.

Eight Questions That Can Help

In this book I detail an approach to evaluation and treatment that in my experience decreases the need for medication, even in children with severe problems. Many kids who come into my office taking one, two, or three psychoactive drugs eventually discontinue them in favor of other means of resolving their difficulties. But I do not mean this as an antidrug polemic. In my experience, families who decide to medicate *after* they have taken the time to examine the available information and nondrug approaches report a much higher level of satisfaction with their choice than those who don't.

One of the strategies I find most useful in weighing a child's individual situation is to ask myself a series of questions, a kind of mental checklist: Is the immediate safety of the child or family in danger? Have appropriate nondrug approaches been given a fair trial? What are the known side effects of the drug this child might receive, and how much remains unknown? And so on. These questions help me slow down and hold the problem up to several different lights before making a recommendation. They help me know each variable more intimately—its weight, its significance to a family and child—before I put it on the scale.

In contemplating this book, I came up with several questions that I felt would be useful for those on the other side of the desk—parents and families who want a firm say in the process. The first part of this book replicates this checklist for you, with each of the following eight chapters organized around one of the questions. In each chapter, I help you understand the major issues underlying the question, arming you with statistics and psychological theory whenever possible. I also show you how real parents and children have responded to these questions, along with their degree of success and satisfaction.

The questions include:

- *Does your child have a disorder?* The word "disorder," like the term "chemical imbalance," is charged with several assumptions that often go unexamined. In this chapter, you'll learn how we arrived at the current biological model of childhood mental illness, in which behavioral or emotional problems are viewed as symptoms of a disorder. You'll also see alternative perspectives that can be useful in caring for difficult children.
- *Has your child received a complete and ethical evaluation?* You may already know from experience that brief evaluations are the norm these days. Unfortunately, this sped-up process often leads to thoughtlessly prescribed medication or to serious problems like learning disabilities being overlooked. When you know what a complete evaluation looks like, you are in a better position to demand one from your practitioner. This chapter also includes tips for helping you find the best doctor or therapist for your child.
- *When time-outs don't work: Have you tried these strategies for effective discipline?* One of the many ironies of parenting is that challenging kids are those who need the most order in their lives. They're also the ones who resist it most aggressively. This chapter shows how one family used methods for limit

setting, structure, and—yes—time-outs to help their children, although those approaches had failed before.

- *Beating Mrs. Bossy and defeating Darth Vader: Can you external-ize the problem?* Here you'll discover a nondrug approach that helps families reframe their child's problem in a way that offers them more power and hope. It often works surprisingly well, especially for kids who are dominated by fears, obsessions, or sensitivities. It doesn't work for every child—nothing, not even medication, can claim to be 100 percent successful—but it can be a rejuvenating exercise for worn-out families, and I have seen it help many children avoid medication altogether.

- *How can teachers and schools help?* Teachers and other school staff, surprisingly, can be surprisingly willing to offer assis-tance. This chapter covers the options available within the regular classroom and in special programs.

- *When is enough enough?* In most cases, it is wise to look at all your options before coming to a decision regarding medica-tion. But sometimes a child's mental state or unavoidable cir-cumstances call out for the particular help that drugs can bring. This chapter helps you identify these conditions.

- *How will the medication affect your child?* This chapter de-scribes the classes of pharmaceuticals most likely to be pre-scribed for children, along with their known and potential benefits and risks. You'll learn how to decipher pharmaceuti-cal claims, and I'll share with you my observations from twenty years of watching how children's bodies and personal-ities react to certain drugs.

- *What if your child won't swallow the pill (and other day-to-day questions when your child is on medication)?* This practical chap-ter anticipates the daily challenges that may arise when psy-chiatric medications are used. What do you tell the child about the drug? How can you tell if the child no longer needs medication? How do you get a fractious child to take a pill in the first place? And so on.

The second part of the book focuses on specific behaviors. The three chapters in this section look at traits that often appear in tandem—aggression, anger, and hyperactivity; shyness, fears, and obsessions; trouble connecting to other people—and show how the strategies outlined in the first part have worked for various children I've seen.

The last chapter of this book is a bit different from the rest. Current professional and popular thinking emphasizes the effects of genetics and biochemistry on children's brains and behavior. Although I do not deny the importance of biological factors, it's critical to remind ourselves that children's brains do not operate in isolation. Our expectations of our children and responses to their actions also have major influence. And we cannot help but be affected by the social, cultural, political, and particularly economic forces that drive the world in which we live. Even if we cannot immediately change our world to the better for our children, our awareness makes such change more likely.

At the very back of the book you'll find a quick guide that lists psychoactive drugs by class and brand name. It is intended to help you locate a specific drug's benefits and known side effects, dosages, and any controversies of which you should be aware.

In the best of worlds, the decision to place a child on medication, or not to, is a matter of art, science, and good intentions. You have already contributed the most important element of the equation—the loving concern that is a child's best therapy. It is my hope that the information and the stories in this book will help you blend hard science with the delicate art of cultivating a child's individual character and temperament. This careful blending is more than just a smart way to help your child. It is a philosophy that rejects mere convenience and speed in favor of moral deliberation about the needs of your child and the world in which she lives.

2

Does Your Child Have a Disorder?

The voice on the other end of the line is gracious, with a slow Virginia drawl that's unusual here in northern California. But it tells the story of a family on the edge. "My daughter is only five years old, and she's already floundering," Carol Huggins tells me. "Michelle won't sit still during story time at her kindergarten, and she gets angry when it's time to stop doing art projects and move on to the next thing. Yesterday she was furious when a little boy wouldn't give up his swing for her, so she pushed him off. The teacher thinks she should have a medical evaluation." At home, Michelle runs around the table during dinner; she won't leave her videos when her parents call. They have tried time-outs and withholding treats when she misbehaves, Carol explains, but they don't want to continue punishing Michelle if she can't help what she's doing. "Can you test her for ADD—or is it ADHD? My sister's older kid is bipolar, and she thinks Michelle might have a chemical imbalance like her son . . . "

In the 1500s, a parent of a rebellious child might have consulted a priest to exorcise a demon from her soul. A century ago, kids who didn't function well in school would work on their parents' farm instead. (If they still didn't behave, they'd likely get a whipping.) In the 1960s, a worried parent might have asked an analyst: Is a repressed trauma disrupting my daughter's psyche?

Now, at the turn of the twenty-first century, Carol asks me if her daughter has a chemical imbalance. That a child's problems are the result of a brain malfunction, rather than an Oedipal complex or a moral defect, is a relatively new idea, but one that has already shaped the vocabulary of American kitchen-table discussions. Phrases that have become common, such as "neurological disorder," "chemical imbalance," and "serotonin insufficiency," all reflect the current philosophy that although some children won't behave, there are others who just can't.

According to popularized versions of biochemical explanations of child behavior, Michelle's problems might be caused by a psychiatric syndrome like attention deficit/hyperactivity disorder (correctly abbreviated as ADHD but also known as ADD). If Michelle "has" ADHD, her activity level and aggression presumably are propelled by neurological forces that she is powerless to resist. Carol believes that the presence or absence of a chemical imbalance will light the way to the fairest means of handling her daughter. If Michelle "has" ADHD, she needs medication and compassion, not punishment. If, on the other hand, Michelle does not have a disorder, medication is useless and nondrug solutions are more fitting.

Carol waits patiently as these musings pass through my head. Her questions imply that there is a clear line in the middle of this new psychiatric landscape: between behavior driven by chemistry and that produced by character; between conditions that are helped by medications and those that are not; between kids who have disorders and those who don't. She wants me to tell her on which side of these lines her daughter is standing.

Sometimes I wish that I could offer Carol and other parents—loving people who would do nearly anything for their children—the comfort of a quick test and brisk diagnosis, with the promise of a pharmaceutical cure. But I entered behavioral pediatrics because I am fascinated by the interaction between hard medical science and the fuzzy, ultimately unknowable nature of humanity. And so I don't believe these sharp lines between disorder and health, or between kids who can't behave and kids who won't, exist.

There are no blood tests, brain scans, or EEGs I can run on Michelle to diagnose her. In an interview, she might demonstrate the six symptoms out of nine that are required for an ADHD diagnosis—but would she really be that much different from a kid who displays only five? Diagnosing psychiatric conditions is at best a subjective endeavor, dependent not just on the observer but on the culture that says "*this* is healthy and *that* is unacceptable."

I, like every other doctor I know, am awed by our steadily increasing knowledge of the human brain. But I am uncomfortable with a purely neurological explanation of childhood problems. I don't believe that human character can be reduced to a series of electrical impulses firing from one neuron to the next; such a philosophy is insufficient for comprehending the mind and soul of a child or anyone else. I think that most of us who have raised children will acknowledge that their environment—home, school, neighborhood, country—has a give-and-take relationship with the personality with which they were born. Biology alone cannot explain what makes us who we are, although it can help.

These days, it's natural for conscientious parents to ask themselves if their child's behavior problems are caused by a disorder. There may not be a yes-or-no answer to that question, but the act of posing it in a reflective manner can give you a window onto the debates that surround it.

Before Biochemistry

Much of the current enthusiasm for biochemistry is a backlash to what came before—Freudian psychoanalytic theory, which held sway in this country from the 1920s through the 1970s. In this model, psychological problems are caused by traumatic childhood experiences, especially those that are pushed down into the unconscious and repressed. Adult treatment takes the form of talk therapy, in which the patient and analyst uncover the repressed information, resulting in the patient's insight and liberation. Kids undergo specialized play therapy with essentially the same goals in mind. Parents, especially mothers, take the heat for the troubles of their offspring. A Freudian analyst might have concluded that Carol was either too cold or too close to her daughter, leaving Michelle stuck in an immature stage of development.

We owe Freud a profound debt for his "discovery" of the unconscious mind and the insight that unspoken and unacknowledged feelings drive our everyday behavior. As a philosophy, his work continues to influence our understanding of art, metaphor, and human conscience. But as a clinical method, the Freudian approach was notorious for its slowness and, ultimately, the lack of evidence for its effectiveness: A person might spend years on the couch without ever seeing improvement. When psychiatric medications like lithium, Thorazine, and tricyclic antidepressants first appeared in the 1950s, producing fast, observable results in patients with serious mental illness, the talk-alone method came under question.

The Freudian paradigm could be overly restrictive too, barring other potentially effective therapies. At the College of Physicians and Surgeons at Columbia University as a medical student in the 1970s, I ran into a few Freudian barriers myself. Once I was treating a ten-year-old boy with a bedwetting problem, and a professor threatened to fail me for advocating the use of a nighttime conditioning machine. My teacher felt that the child's problem stemmed from watching his parents perform the sex act and would hear of no treatment other than play therapy to work through the trauma. I felt the child was being denied a treatment that was backed up by good evidence.

In the second half of the twentieth century, American psychiatry, still dominated by Freudians, found itself in serious danger of losing credibility as a science and a branch of medicine. Other members of the medical establishment could perceive little of the scientific method at work in Freudian talk therapy. Another locus of complaints was the *Diagnostic and Statistical Manual* (DSM), the bible of psychiatric academicians. The DSM categorized psychological ailments along with their Freudian explanations—an apparently scientific undertaking. But the entries were so vague that almost any set of problems could easily fit two, three, or more diagnoses. It was impossible to standardize research on this slippery basis; without objective markers of illness or successful treatment, academic and research psychiatrists feared the loss of the respect, prestige, and money granted to other branches of medicine.

Embracing the Brain

By the 1970s, in what appeared to be a 180-degree turn, American psychiatry rejected the experience-based trauma model of Freud and embraced a biological and genetic philosophy of childhood disorders. As a result, its tenuous foothold in academia and the sciences has been restored—at least for the time being. Psychiatry continues to be discreetly belittled and stigmatized by the rest of medicine, a situation that impels the ongoing quest for biochemical and "hard" explanations of behavior.

Psychiatry's forays into brain science were undertaken primarily by working backward from the drugs known to have an effect on behavior and emotions. In previous decades, all we knew was that certain psychoactive drugs worked—*how* they worked was a mystery. Then psychiatrists became scientists in a more traditional sense, trying to analyze a drug's particular mechanism of action and tracing its path through the nervous system.

That's a whopping task, as there are an estimated 1 trillion nerve cells in the mature brain. At best, we are wending our way through a dark labyrinth, guided only by the light of a match. So far, we've mapped out a couple of twists and turns of the maze and ruled out some dead ends. But we don't fully understand any of the existing psychiatric drugs. And the overarching design of the brain remains elusive. As John Horgan eloquently states in his book *The Undiscovered Mind:* "Scientists may never completely succeed in healing, replicating, or explaining the human mind. Our minds may always remain, to some extent, undiscovered."

What we have learned, however, is that our battery of psychiatric drugs seems to work mainly by its effects on neurotransmitters, chemicals that facilitate the transmission of electrical impulses from one nerve cell to another. The neurotransmitters adrenaline, norepinephrine, dopamine, and serotonin have all been associated with certain mental states. And we've found that particular areas of the brain are linked to specific behaviors, at least some of the time: Activity in the frontal lobes of the cerebral cortex is associated with impulsivity and attention problems; in the parietal lobes, a higher level of activity is connected with obsession and worrying.

I'm sure that Freud himself would be enthralled by the current research. But in our intoxication with these discoveries, we may have forgotten how little we still understand.

What Do We Mean When We Say "Disorder"?

When you turn on a news program or talk show and hear physicians, psychiatrists, and parent advocates using the term "disorder," what are they really saying?

Most of them are influenced by the brain-based research that looks to chemical interpretations of behavior and emotions. The word sounds so official, so unquestionably medical, that to question its use is to risk sounding like a throwback to the days when mental illness was considered a sign of moral turpitude. But I worry that the assumptions underpinning this and other terms currently in vogue are based on an overly simplified interpretation of the existing research, one that denies the staggering complexity of biochemistry, not to mention the richness of human experience itself. Here are a few assumptions that can affect how your child is diagnosed and treated.

Fallacy 1: If a Child Meets a Standardized Set of Psychological Criteria, the Child Has a Disorder

When teachers or others suggest that a child "get tested" for a psychological problem, they usually mean that a doctor or therapist should check for the existence of symptoms listed in the *Diagnostic and Statistical Manual.* Since the DSM often forms the sole basis for a child's diagnosis these days, I think it's worth a closer look.

As I already mentioned, the DSM came under fire during Freudian days for its vagueness. In 1980, a revised DSM was published that expelled Freudian notions of causality (anxiety is caused by an overprotective mother), instead favoring lists of behaviors that characterized each disorder (anxiety is characterized by excessive anxiety and worry for at least six months, difficulty controlling the worry, and so on). These symptoms theoretically could be observed and counted, satisfying the discipline's need for more "science."

This new DSM was primarily meant for academicians, who sorely needed a way to standardize their research. I remember, as a young doctor, leafing through the book with approval; I thought a neutral, descriptive system was an improvement over the earlier version and could be a useful tool in research studies. But the book is also used by doctors and psychiatrists in a clinical setting. If a child in the doctor's office meets a minimum number of symptoms, he is a candidate for a certain psychiatric syndrome—but does not necessarily "have" it. Ideally, the doctor will conduct interviews with the child, his parents, and teachers to come to a rounded understanding of the patient and his world.

But doctors nowadays are heavily influenced by the biological model of childhood problems. This model, which points to the brain as the source of all difficulties, does not take into account the child's environment. In addition, even the most careful doctors are under pressure from insurance companies and government agencies that use DSM labels as the dividing line between kids who receive reimbursement or special school services and kids who don't.

Under the pressure and philosophy of current practice, a doctor may simply run down the list of symptoms with a parent or teacher: "Does your child have difficulty awaiting his turn seldom, often, or never? Does he interrupt or intrude on others seldom, often, or never?" The answers are then tallied up and a diagnosis is made. A computer or layperson could just as easily perform the evaluation. The child himself is observed only minimally by the doctor; rarely is the context of his behavior—family life, school, friendships—considered.

The tidy list of DSM symptoms may look objective, and they may satisfy the discipline's need to look "scientific," but they are heavily subject to the eye of the beholder. If I attempt to diagnose Michelle according to the DSM criteria for attention deficit/hyperactivity disorder, I may ask Carol how frequently her daughter fidgets with her hands or feet—seldom, often, or never? And she would be justified in responding (as the television character Tony Soprano famously demanded of his son's school psychologist), "What's a fidget?" Or, "What's the difference between *often* and *seldom?*" And isn't there a normal amount of fidgeting among small children in school?

When I am talking with Carol about whether her daughter talks or runs about excessively—behaviors that are also symptoms of ADHD—I must remind myself that every person's answers are colored by an individual sense of what's average or appropriate. Studies show that depressed mothers tend to overreport their children's problems and that general education teachers rank the same behaviors as more troublesome than special education teachers do. And none of us maintains consistency among our own rankings. If I ask parents to fill out a DSM-based questionnaire and then, two weeks later, ask them to fill it out again, they will report fewer problems—even if their child hasn't received any form of treatment whatsoever.

Despite calls from the American Psychiatric Association and the American Academy of Pediatrics for doctors to slow down the evaluation process, to take more time interviewing children and the important adults in their lives, this rather cold and quick approach to diagnosis continues to be all too common. So when the result of a checklist-style evaluation is that a child is labeled with a disorder, I wonder how much we've really learned about that child. Perhaps the process of diagnosing by the DSM tells us more about ourselves—something to keep in mind when a doctor opens up that big block of book.

Fallacy 2: If a Child Is Diagnosed with a Disorder, the Child Has a Chemical Imbalance

So far, there is no good research proving that any psychiatric syndrome is caused by a deficiency of certain neurotransmitters or unusual blood-flow patterns or any other brain malfunction. The common perception that depression, anxiety, ADHD, or any other psychiatric condition is clearly caused by a "chemical imbalance" stems from a logical error that I describe in more detail below.

Fallacy 3: A Psychiatric Drug That "Works" Is Proof That the Problematic Behavior Was Caused by a Chemical Imbalance

This is the logic that says, If a medication that increases available serotonin (Prozac is such a drug) makes a depressed person feel better, then an insufficient amount of serotonin is a cause of the depression. The depression was caused by a "brain disorder." The same fallacy holds for Ritalin and hyperactivity—if Ritalin helps a child settle down, the child must have an imbalance that is corrected by the medication.

But the science does not back up such definitive statements. If a person with a headache improves with aspirin, we do not therefore conclude that the pain was caused by an aspirin deficiency. Yet that's the same logical leap made by those who believe that the benefits of psychoactive drugs prove the existence of a chemical imbalance. In truth, Ritalin and similar medications have been shown to heighten the alertness and focus of almost anyone who takes an appropriate amount, whether the recipient is a hyper kid or an adult chess master. Other psychiatric drugs, like Prozac, have a similarly broad effect on those who are struggling and those who are adequately coping.

Fallacy 4: If My Child Has a Disorder, Psychiatric Drugs Are the Only Effective Treatment

Perhaps the most exciting discovery that brain science has made in recent years is that our nervous system is plastic, meaning that it can be reshaped by behavioral interventions as well as by drugs. So even if we postulate that childhood disorders are caused by brain chemistry, we may be able to alter that chemistry via drug-free therapies.

One UCLA study followed a group of patients who met the DSM criteria for obsessive-compulsive disorder. Brain scans had shown that in these patients, rates of glucose metabolism were higher than usual in the parietal lobes. The patients were divided into two sets. The first received drug therapy and the second went through desensitization training—for instance, a person afraid of going on a plane would first look at photos of a plane, then watch a film about one, then visit the airport, and finally board a plane for a trip. At the end of the study, both groups showed a reduction of bothersome symptoms. But the real surprise came when the scientists ran a final set of brain scans. The patients who had received drug therapy now had normal levels of brain activity, *but so did the patients who received a purely behavioral intervention.* I saw photos of the two sets of scans, in which the brain looked like a walnut. In both sets, the edges of the walnuts—the parietal lobes—were no longer white, a marker of high activity. They were gray or dark, just like the rest of the brain. I can recall marveling: Here's clear evidence that both medications *and* environment can alter biochemistry.

This finding, as well as research across many fields of medicine, strongly suggests that both biochemistry and environment participate in multiple feedback loops throughout the central nervous system, shaping each other in the process. So to approach "disorders" as purely genetic or inherently neurological malfunctions that can be treated only with medications is to ignore the cutting edge of neuroscience itself.

Developments in neuroscience call on us to shift out of black-and-white thinking, the kind that says, Child X is biologically impaired and needs medication, but Child Y is just a rotten kid who should be packed off to boarding school. Instead, we need to think about how both biology *and* environment can intersect to cause problems—and to solve them.

Temperament/Fit: Another View of Children's Behavior

One way of thinking about kids' behavior problems has been especially useful to me in my daily practice. It blends biology with environment, offering parents some causes for their child's baffling behavior *and* holding out hope for positive change. It's called the temperament/fit theory and may sound like common sense—the kind of wisdom your grandmother might have handed down.

In the 1950s, child psychiatrists Stella Chess, Alexander Thomas, and Herbert Birch were inspired by their own children to consider whether some personality traits are inborn—rather than determined by early childhood experiences, as the Freudian model claimed. They conducted a large-scale study of several hundred children and identified categories of temperament, the basic disposition that is an inherent part of a child's constitution from birth. Their three categories—which are admittedly large and loose—are *easy, difficult,* and *sensitive.*

Easy children adapt to change fairly quickly; they are even-tempered, flexible kids who can wake up from naps and move from class to recess and back again without an undue amount of fuss. Just watching these easy kids in restaurants, where they sit happily noshing on their fish sticks, can give parents of more challenging kids—who are emptying the salt and pepper shakers from their table or keening because they don't want to even *look* at tartar sauce—a pang of envy.

Sensitive kids have more dramatic responses, both physiologically and behaviorally, to stimuli in the environment. Change a sensitive child's diaper, and he might turn red or pale; introduce him to a stranger and he'll practically try to crawl back into your womb. Bright lights, loud noises, and strong odors all affect sensitive children powerfully. It may be hard to get your sensitive child to sleep through the night, and these kids may demand a routine, like the same clothes day after day.

Like sensitive children, *difficult* kids may respond fiercely to low-level changes in their environment. Difficult children, however, are also persistent, intense, and impulsive. If the kid doesn't like having his diaper changed, he'll let you know it with howls that may last right through the next changing time, despite your best attempts at consolation. If he wants something, he *needs* to eat, and *now,* Mommy! It's hard to hold out against such a child; his impulses (and lung power) might be much stronger than your willingness to endure an explosive tantrum, especially in public. Difficult kids may also have trouble adapting to new circumstances. It's not easy for them to shift into a less active gear when lunchtime or recess is over and it's time to return to a quiet activity. They may not sleep or eat on regular schedules, and, like Michelle, they might be challenged by classroom routines.

"Goodness of Fit"

One appealing aspect of the temperament/fit philosophy is that it does not view difficult or sensitive temperaments as inherently pathological. According to this philosophy, Michelle's persistence and aggression are not the symptoms of a disorder. Instead, they occupy a place on the long, long continuum of possible behaviors, as a living example of human variety and range. A world without Michelles might be more peaceful, but it would hardly be as interesting.

I think Carol would be relieved that the temperament/fit theory avoids the kind of parent blaming that dominated the Freudian view. Kids are *born* with tendencies toward difficult or sensitive traits; they demonstrate them within the first hours of life. Perhaps our increasingly sophisticated science will one day locate biological or genetic markers in the brains or DNA of these kids. In this model, biology—although it forms the foundation of personality—is not a life sentence. A child's happiness or success depends less on the traits he is born with than on what Chess and her colleagues called "goodness of fit" with family, neighborhood, schools, and the culture as a whole. If a kid's temperament matches the expectations and responses of his environment, life is going to be fairly harmonious. But if the environment places heavy demands on the child without giving him the support to meet those challenges, there will likely be stress, conflict, and behavior problems.

When I think about the problem of "good fit" with a child's environment, I am often reminded of Jenny, a sweet, dreamy child of fourteen who was well-liked but performed poorly in school. Her parents, who wanted her to attend college and climb the career ladder, felt that her future was in jeopardy. Jenny wanted to please her parents but couldn't seem to work up interest in her assignments; nor did she have a particular aptitude for scholarly activity. I couldn't help wondering if she was merely a child out of time, a girl who would have flourished on a farm a hundred years ago. She could have left school after learning the basics and assisted her mother with chores at home, in preparation for one day running a household of her own. By no means am I suggesting that girls are better off in the kitchen than in the classroom—merely that it is possible to imagine an environment in which this specific child would have been a star of the community rather than a candidate for medication. In turn, there are surely many girls today whose academic leanings would have made life difficult for them a century ago.

Now let's consider Michelle, who at first glance appears to exhibit the traits of a difficult child. She lives in an upper-middle-class American home. In order to send her to a good school and give her material comforts, both her parents work and must therefore order their lives according to a strict schedule. She goes to an academic kindergarten with large classrooms, where she must adjust quickly from one activity to another. In this environment, her persistent, impulsive temperament has already become the source of frustration and clashes. Yet studies by Michael Rutter, child psychiatrist emeritus of the United Kingdom, show that in some circumstances Michelle's hot temper might work in her favor. Rutter looked at African children during a famine and determined that those who cried and created more of a fuss—difficult children—were fed more often than easy babies. In this environment, a difficult temperament confers a distinct survival advantage. Presumably, the traits of difficult and sensitive children exist because in the past they possessed evolutionary benefits that may still be important. We cannot predict very well what skills and talents will be valuable ten years from now. Consider the rise of the "nerds"—successful adults who might have seemed a poor fit with the social milieu of their childhood.

I have found that imagining how kids like Michelle or Jenny might fare in another time or place can be a useful exercise, especially when parents are concerned that their child is simply bad or diseased. I believe that we all need to ask ourselves whether the crowded classrooms, exhausted families, and intense pace and competition of American life are heaping too great a burden on our children. My previous book, *Running on Ritalin,* was written in part to voice these concerns. However, my immediate job as a doctor, and yours as a parent, is less one of social criticism than of assisting a specific child who must live within a given society.

Should Michelle's parents feel guilty that a famine isn't providing an environment in which their daughter's traits allow her to shine? Should Jenny's parents give her the all-clear to drop out (as long as she puts dinner on the table each night)?

Of course not. The challenge of living inside a family, a neighborhood, a school, and a culture is one that we all must face; learning family rules and negotiating the demands of community life are among the great duties and pleasures of humanity. But some of our children are going to need extra assistance as they learn how to "fit" without sacrificing their unique personalities. It helps to have some awareness that a child's current problems are also a reflection of a struggle that many of us share with larger social-cultural demands.

As I think about the nature of our kids' problems, I am reminded of the work of George Engels, a thoughtful internist who wrote extensively from the 1960s to the 1980s about the interaction between nature and nurture. He proposed that the purely medical model of disease—not just psychiatric disease but "classic" illnesses such as pneumonia or ear infections—failed to take into account the emotional and social factors that contributed to the problem. Interest in Engels's work peaked just before the revolutionary and "scientific" DSM was published. It is ironic that American psychiatry, rather than lead the rest of medicine to adopt a more wholistic view of disease, opted for the medical model in order to protect its status as a science.

Helping Michelle Find a Fit

When I talk to Carol and her husband after evaluating Michelle, it's possible my opener would go something like this:

"Yes, Michelle would meet some doctor's DSM criteria for attention deficit/hyperactivity disorder, combined type. That label can be useful if it gets her special services at school or if it will persuade your insurance company to pay for our meetings.

"But in our conversations, I'd prefer not to use a label when describing Michelle. I think that focuses us too much on what's *wrong* and presents her in terms of a stereotype or disease. Instead, I'd prefer to describe your daughter in all her strengths and weaknesses. Let's characterize her in more neutral terms: energetic, intense, persistent, and resistant toward change. Some of those qualities make her the active, irrepressible girl you love. But you know firsthand that they also make her a difficult child to raise; it's especially hard for her to fit into the structure of school."

Describing Michelle and the problem in this way interprets her behavior as a normal variation of personality that fits poorly into the environment. This doesn't mean that Michelle does not have some big problems, but it is a striking conceptual difference from "Michelle has a disorder." Because it acknowledges both inborn traits and environmental factors, such a description allows for a wider variety of interventions. It is likely that Michelle's parents and I will discuss ways to help her prepare for transitions and to address her impulsivity. We will look at her environment: What is reasonable to expect of her? Certainly Michelle's parents can—and should—require her to sit down at the dinner table and to refrain from violent behavior. She will "fit" better with parents who make the rules clear and give her more attention, more immediacy, and more consistency.

Michelle's school environment may be part of the larger picture, with its large classrooms and lengthy curricula. Perhaps her teachers have received in-service training programs that encourage them to view many kinds of child behavior as potential ADHD. In that case, a visit to the school to organize a behavioral program for Michelle would be in order, and if that fails, switching classes or even schools could be considered.

We'll need to talk more about life at home—are there financial troubles, marital tensions, or conflicting attitudes toward discipline that may be contributing to Michelle's difficulties? What are some examples of times when family members—including Michelle—have worked well together, and what can we learn from them? We can also think about activities for Michelle—perhaps martial arts, swimming, or gymnastics—that play to her strengths and give her a sense of accomplishment. After all that, if Michelle is still struggling, there may be a place for using a psychiatric drug sensibly.

When I decide to prescribe a drug, I try to make it clear that I am not "curing" a child's "disorder" as much as I am making accessible another tool to help the child behave the way he would like to. Sometimes drugs can jump-start children who are at risk for giving up on themselves or are starting to hang out with kids who take advantage of their poor self-image. In a pinch, drugs can help a child remain in a regular classroom or school when no other option is available for parents—in other words, they're another way of achieving a good fit.

But drugs do not teach children, parents, or teachers coping strategies; they merely give them a hand up. If I were to prescribe medication for Michelle, I would ask her parents to continue behavioral interventions as well as the drug regimen. Otherwise, she—and they—may begin to feel that she can't succeed without pharmaceuticals. Although this may be true for a very small group of kids, I am optimistic that most children, even those with serious behavior and emotional problems, can learn skills to help them succeed, very often without any medication at all.

3

Has Your Child Received a Complete and Ethical Evaluation?

A mother once told me about a telephone call she made to a specialist regarding her daughter's disruptive behavior. The doctor told her to fill out a questionnaire he was sending via mail and to have the girl's teacher fill out one as well. In return for the completed forms, he mailed the woman a prescription for Ritalin. He never saw the child or the parent!

I am not personally acquainted with any physicians who advocate this kind of practice. It would fling the doors wide open to malpractice lawsuits, not to mention that it is probably illegal. But I'm afraid this outrageous story is simply an extreme example of a definite trend: speedy, by-the-numbers evaluations in which doctors simply check off symptoms in the DSM list and tally them up. Specialists like behavioral pediatricians or psychiatrists typically take just *one* forty-five-to fifty-minute evaluation before drawing a conclusion. Most of that time is spent talking with a parent (usually just the mother); a brief period is devoted to a meeting with the child. When the doctor involved is not a specialist but a primary-care physician, an evaluation may take no more than twenty or thirty minutes. To my mind, the quickie evaluation is unethical. It cuts corners, mostly for the sake of speed and money, and it tilts the treatment toward medication, which may deliver short-term changes but raises major questions about long-term effectiveness and safety. Nor is medication the moral equivalent to better parenting and education for the child.

Before you stand behind a diagnosis of your child, you may wish to ask yourself whether she has received a complete and ethical evaluation, one that evolves over several visits and encompasses much more than symptom counting. A truly thorough evaluation may cost more than a quick visit, and it certainly takes more time, but I've found that it results in much greater satisfaction for the parents and the child. A slower, more considered exploration of the child and her world will naturally lead to a fruitful discussion of both drug and nondrug interventions, instead of a doctor automatically reaching for a prescription pad.

In this chapter, I tell the story of the Gardner family and show how their evaluation unfolded. Their story is striking for the intense estrangement and hostility between the boy's mother and father. Although it is not unusual for behavioral problems to surface amid marital tensions, I am by no means suggesting that kids' difficulties are *always* a reflection of troubles at home. Indeed, raising a challenging child can strain marital relationships. I am sharing this story because it demonstrates how an inadequate evaluation could easily miss obvious environmental factors that contribute to a child's behavior; it also highlights certain priorities of mine, such as having both parents involved in diagnosis and treatment. Other circumstances of the Gardners' case, such as a buried learning disability, are vivid reminders of how important it is to conduct a thorough examination before coming to a conclusion.

Getting Dads Involved

I first spoke with Holly Gardner, Reese's mother, on the telephone. Holly explained to me that Reese, who was nearly seven, experienced behavior problems at school and had trouble finishing his work. His teacher had suggested that Reese "get tested" for ADHD during his summer break. So far, our conversation was much like several others I have during a typical week. It wasn't until I inquired about Reese's father that alarm bells started ringing in my head.

Holly's voice tightened at my question. She explained that she had separated from Reese's father, Ari, two years ago, and the divorce had just become final. Ari and Holly had joint legal and physical custody; Reese spent one week with one of his parents and the subsequent week with the other. "But Ari wouldn't be interested in talking to you," she said. "He might even try to stop Reese from seeing you, and I can't let that happen."

Although most evaluations these days begin with a phone call from the child's mother, I strongly believe that *both* parents—married, divorced, or separated, as long as each has an active connection with the child—must be involved. When mother and father are part of the evaluation, I receive an expanded view of the child's world, along with a more appropriate set of potential solutions.

The mother, even in these times, is most often the first parent to contact me (perhaps because schools tend to contact mothers about problems first, even when both parents work). If she tells me that the child's father can't or won't appear at the first session, I explain my feelings and try to brainstorm with her for solutions. If the father is busy at work, I often suggest a meeting at the beginning or end of the day, when schedules tend to be more flexible. If the father doesn't believe the child has any real problems, I say that it's even *more* important for him to come in. When parents disagree over how to handle a problem, or whether a problem really exists in the first place, it's critically important for me to hear from both of them. If the mother tells me that the father is deeply recalcitrant, I ask permission to call him directly. In my twenty years of practice I can count on fewer than ten fingers the number of fathers who refused to see me at least once. On those occasions, I've still learned a great deal about the family and can almost guarantee that the biggest problem in the family is between the parents and not with the child.

When Holly told me that Ari not only was uninterested in the evaluation but actively opposed it, I decided to tread carefully. She was so obviously tense at the mere mention of her ex-husband's name that I first invited her to come in alone. I knew we could better discuss in person whether Ari should be involved.

The Initial Consultation

The first component of a complete evaluation is a history of the problem. I prefer to get this information without the child present, since it's hard for parents to talk when a kid is squirming or asking to play with the toys that are on my shelves. I also dislike the typical practice of speaking explicitly about a child's problems in front of her, as if the child were a piece of furniture with no feelings. I very much want to see the family in action later on, and I need to hear about the problems directly from the child. But first, I want the parents' uninhibited view.

Holly, a tall, willowy woman of about forty, entered my office and shook my hand. She was dressed in a jacket and skirt for her public relations job. She looked professional, but I sensed vulnerability from the get-go.

Holly sat down at the edge of her chair. "Reese doesn't do what he doesn't want to do, at school or at home. His first-grade teacher told me that she's been having problems with Reese, mostly with getting him to do his work. He can also be disruptive, and she thinks he's hyper." Holly went on to explain that Reese had been slower to read and spell than the other kids in his class, although he seemed to be getting the hang of it by the end of the school year.

I asked her for examples of the problems at home. Holly rolled her eyes. "He tests me on everything. *Everything* is a battle." If she didn't sit next to him when it was time for homework, he would sneak out of the room to watch TV or play with the dog. Getting ready for school in the morning was the same story. She had to go into his room several times to wake him up, even though they both knew he was just lying awake in bed. He turned on the television when he was supposed to be eating breakfast and then wouldn't pull himself away from his show to get dressed. They ended up screaming at each other, with Holly literally jamming his shoes onto his feet. Sometimes Reese hit her. Holly stopped to take a breath. "Could he be ADD?"

Clearly, Reese exhibited some serious problems at Holly's house, the hitting being the most disturbing. But Holly had not yet described many examples of the impulsive, inattentive, or hyperactive behaviors that are the cornerstones of the ADHD diagnosis. Instead, what I heard made me think of a kid who was challenging, intense, and determined. As our conversation continued, I asked her if Reese could focus for long periods of time on activities he liked, apart from video games, which seem designed for the hyperactive mind. According to Holly, Reese could play up to an hour by himself with K'nex (a kind of construction set) or Transformer robots. Although being able to stick with enjoyable pursuits doesn't necessarily rule out hyperactivity or inattentiveness, I know that I am dealing with a very impaired kid when a patient can't even focus on fun pastimes. Reese, luckily, wasn't in that category of severity.

Later in the discussion, Holly added, "But sometimes Reese can switch activities very quickly. And he's so hyper, especially after he comes back from the week at his father's." After returning to her house, Reese was jumpy, spending just a few minutes with one toy before abandoning it and moving on to another. Even television would fail to hold his attention. He became even more obstinate, refusing to come to the dinner table—an otherwise unusual circumstance for her always hungry boy.

Such behavior is a familiar pattern; kids on transfers often seem "wired" or more intense for a day or two after the switch. Again, I felt that these weren't signs of hyperactivity so much as further examples of an easily frustrated, determined child, one who was apparently struggling during transition periods.

At this point, it might have been possible for me to put Reese into a psychiatric category. Whether he met the criteria for ADHD was still unclear, but he did fit the description of oppositional defiant disorder (ODD), a syndrome characterized by angry disobedience, and possibly even bipolar disorder. Too many evaluations these days would have stopped here, and Holly would have left clutching a prescription. But a complete evaluation asks for more from both the parents and the clinician. And so Holly and I began to talk about the divorce.

It had been ugly, with prolonged litigation over financial issues and custody of Reese. Two years after the initial separation, Holly told me that she still felt harassed by Ari. He left angry ten-minute messages on her answering machine, blaming Holly for her inability to control their son, wanting to change the time and place for Reese's drop-off, telling Holly that she needed to change her scheduled vacation, or asking for more money. At first, Ari picked Reese up at her house, but he often yelled at her and, according to Holly, had once held the outside of her house door closed so that she couldn't leave.

Holly had begun talking about Ari by giving me an intense stare and a look of disgust. But soon, sadness and resignation softened her features. "Now we exchange Reese every week at a McDonald's parking lot. I told him we had to communicate through a written ledger instead of speaking. I guess I've never been very good at standing up for myself. I just try to ignore his phone messages and hope that he'll leave me alone."

But the more Holly tried to hide, the more Ari pursued. His ledger entries consisted of pages and pages criticizing Holly's parenting. And he began sending her certified letters threatening to sue for more custody.

Holly was convinced that Ari would try to block an evaluation of Reese, and she expected him to reject any possibility of ADHD in his child. She also feared that he would use the boy's school problems and her consultation with me as proof that she was an incompetent parent. I could see that she was truly frightened, but I had to tell her the truth:

Without Ari's knowledge or permission, I doubted I could do much good for her son. I gave her several reasons. For one, my evaluation would be incomplete, possibly inaccurate, because I'd miss out on the view of one of the two most important people in Reese's life.

"But the most important issue," I explained, "is that an angry, antagonistic parent could effectively undo weeks of my treatment and all of your efforts in just one weekend with his son. If Reese comes to see me with you, it could become an act of disloyalty to his father. If we decide Reese should have medication, the simple act of his taking a pill could have the same consequences."

Holly reluctantly agreed to let me call Ari after she sent him a note to let him know that we had met. I took a deep breath before I picked up the telephone; however, my short talk with Ari went smoothly. He immediately agreed to come in and speak with me about Reese. This short encounter illustrates one of the reasons getting professional help can be useful: Outsiders like me aren't bound by the unspoken but powerful "family rules." In this case, the "rule" was that Ari would reject any entreaty, hurting the entreator in the process. As an outsider, I cared less about the rule and about being hurt than Holly did, and this attitude was probably reflected in my approach to Ari. (But I am not always successful. All of us, even professionals, have our own hangups and rules that can cause us to be influenced by the family.)

Ari Gardner was a trim, impeccably tailored man with dark good looks. When he arrived in my office for his visit, he smiled and complimented me for reaching out to him. But once we began talking, Ari's voice took on a darker aspect and he began to speak excitedly. His entire body tensed as he leaned forward in his seat, stabbing his finger at me for emphasis.

"I don't buy this stuff about ADHD. Reese is much closer to me than to Holly. *I* don't have trouble with him. The school doesn't call *me* to complain when he's at *my* house. Now she's trying to blame her own inadequacies on ADHD and is willing to medicate the boy to make her point." Although Ari was angry and apparently trying to intimidate me, I appreciated his directness. I also was sympathetic with his reluctance to put Reese on psychoactive medications.

"He doesn't always listen to me, either," Ari said, turning his palms up, "but that's not especially abnormal for a boy." He acknowledged that Reese had some problems "minding and doing his work at school," but Ari had a different take on the teacher's analysis. According to him, Reese's teacher felt the problems were "manageable."

I reminded Ari that by staying involved, he'd have more influence over the process. After some more talk and considerable fuming, he agreed to come in again with Reese. But he made it clear that he was still skeptical.

The Family Interview

I have found that the family interview, in which everyone who lives in the child's home—parents, siblings, grandparents, anyone—comes in for one forty-five minute visit, is the single most useful component of my evaluation. (When a child lives in two different homes because of a divorce, I ask that each family come in separately, so that I can see the child in her usual environments.) My insistence on the family interview developed from my training at the Child Study Unit at the University of California–San Francisco, which emphasized the importance of seeing a child in his environment as part of a multifaceted approach to treatment. This might sound like common sense, but it was still radical in the 1970s, when Freudian thought continued to dominate pediatric psychology. Today, it flies in the face of our obsession with biochemically oriented theory.

When I meet with a family, I can point out their strengths as a group and note some of the difficulties. Perhaps more important, the parents and I develop a certain bond once we've all experienced the child's behavior unfold in real time. Sometimes what I discover helps me see the family in a new, enlightening way. I once worked with a twelve-year-old boy who constantly argued with his parents and had failed two subjects the previous semester. But when the entire family came in, it was his six-year-old sister who was out of control, racing around the room and taunting Bennett. He would insult her cruelly, calling her a dweeb and a twerp and mocking her drawings. Since she was too little to respond with equivalent verbal attacks, she either tried to scratch him or screamed for her parents. I got a strong sense of how difficult life was for this entire family; I could also see that the boy's failure to handle his sister's provocations suggested just how fragile and lacking in confidence he was. I was worried about the effects of his repeated attacks on the little girl, but I also appreciated that she was a major pain. Our future work together would have to include helping the parents handle the girl's inflammatory behavior and helping Bennett find some alternative means of responding to her.

As schedules had it, I wound up meeting Reese first with his father. My office consists of three rooms: the waiting room, a rather large and spartan family room where kids can spread out and play on the floor without bumping into one another (it's also childproofed so that the adults can talk without having to supervise toddlers), and another, smaller room where either the family or I can talk and play with the children. In this room, a wall of shelves filled with little figures and miniature toys lines the back wall. Reese came bounding into the family room of my office without waiting for his father or for an introduction. He made a beeline for the toys he saw in the playroom, but one sharp bark from Ari brought Reese heeling to the couch.

Reese sat down, and for the first time I had a chance to observe him physically. He was a boy of medium build with sandy-colored hair—a normal-looking kid, but one who had a perpetual frown on his face. The three of us were able to talk seriously for about fifteen minutes, despite some interruptions from Reese. Not fantastic, but not bad for a seven-year-old.

However, I did notice a pattern in Ari's conversation with Reese. It went something like this:

"If you know your teacher will be angry, why don't you finish your work at school?" asked Ari.

"I don't know," Reese said.

"Well, do you *try?*"

"Yes," Reese said, rather matter-of-factly.

"Can you try harder?"

"I don't know."

"You know you'll get punished if you don't behave, right? So why don't you?"

"I don't know. Can we play now?"

I suspected that Ari and Reese had reenacted this type of conversation many times. Ari confirmed it with a heavy nod. He was trying to corner his son with verbal logic, but Reese—who was perfectly capable of answering the questions—correctly sensed a trap. He evaded his father with the time-honored kid's strategy of acting dumb. Ari's grilling may have been intended to direct Reese toward an understanding of the problem, but it came off more like a power game, much like the kind of tactics Holly had complained about.

From what I'd heard from Holly, and from what I'd seen of Ari already, I might have expected him to be an authoritarian, controlling parent. But as Ari and Reese played with the games on my shelves, a curious duet developed. Ari would hold up one toy for Reese's approval—which Reese would waffle over and then reject. Then he'd select another, and then another, with the same results. Ari, it turned out, was actually quite deferential to his son. When Reese launched a Lincoln Log as a catapult, Ari gently asked him not to. Reese continued to send Lincoln Logs flying across my office, with Ari ineffectually saying, "I don't think you should do that anymore." It wasn't until one of the logs nearly hit me that Ari abruptly got up and roughly swept the toys away from his son. Reese was momentarily cowed, but then he went on to something else.

Ari was a commanding presence, but he appeared to avoid conflicts with Reese. I wondered if he feared that placing limits on Reese would cause his son to prefer Holly. I made a note to myself: How much of Reese's behavior was an attempt to get his parents to demonstrate their strength and consistency, to prove that there was security in his constantly shifting world?

Later that week, Holly and Reese came in for their family meeting. Our conversation went more smoothly than it had with Ari. This time, Reese managed twenty minutes of talk quite easily. Mother and son were clearly comfortable together; theirs was a more open dialogue of problems at school and at home. In contrast to his repeated "I don't knows" with his father, Reese told his mother and me that it was "the pits" when his parents argued. He said his dad "was mean." I took his comments seriously but appreciated the particular audience with whom he was sharing this opinion.

I set out a large sheet of paper on the coffee table and asked Holly and Reese to draw a picture together without speaking. This exercise and other games like puppet shows help me appreciate family dynamics. Once a kid climbed up on the table and sat on the paper so that no one else could draw on "his" space (the entire sheet)—a literally graphic representation of the power he held over his family! Holly and Reese's drawing experience was not quite so dramatic, but it did showcase Reese's characteristics of intensity and persistence. When Holly mistakenly changed his tank into a car, he howled. During their play with toys, Reese grew very bossy, pulling box after box of figures from the shelf and ignoring his mother's admonitions to pick up the ones he left scattered on the floor. Reese was also far more critical of Holly than of his father. "Stop it!" he shouted, when she changed the direction of the train they were playing with. If Reese carried this sort of behavior into the classroom, I mused, he would not be appreciated by either his teacher or his peers. The next step in the evaluation was for me to call Reese's school.

Communicating with Professionals

In 1998 the National Institutes of Health Consensus Conference on ADHD concluded that a "structural divide" exists between teachers who originate complaints about children's behavior and performance in school and the doctors who evaluate and make treatment suggestions. In fact, a study from the 1970s showed that teachers were 50 percent more likely to carry out a doctor's recommendations when the doctor appeared at a school meeting.

Parents like Holly are left as go-betweens to report a teacher's suspicions to the doctor or to inform a teacher of the doctor's findings. When parents disagree about a child's problems, as Holly and Ari did, the potential for miscommunication in this game of "telephone" is multiplied.

A solution that many doctors rely on nowadays is the mailed-in questionnaire directed to the teacher. They're certainly convenient, and they offer a modicum of standardization to the process, but I find them inadequate. Few questionnaires cover ground aside from the child's weaknesses, and the slanted emphasis puts everyone into a negative and alarmist mind-set. Nor does a questionnaire tell me anything about a teacher's practices and opinions. Teachers, like the rest of us, are humans whose observations are influenced by their personal style and situation. One teacher's behavior problem is another teacher's at times exasperating but good-natured clown. And so I believe that direct telephone contact between doctor and teacher is essential. We talk about how the teacher runs the classroom, the teacher's feelings about psychiatric diagnoses, and her opinions on the use of medication in children. It may take a few days of phone tag to get in touch, but a respectful one-on-one exchange can tell me a lot about the child's life from nine in the morning until three in the afternoon.

I spoke with Reese's teacher, Mrs. Leslie, over the telephone. She felt Reese had made great progress over the year; he had started out as a virtual nonreader and before summer vacation could decode most first-grade words. At that point, though, he was still one of the weaker readers in his class. She thought he participated well in class discussion and said he was a good artist. But she had a very difficult time keeping Reese on task. He played with his pencils, rocked in his chair, talked to his neighbors, and at times outright refused to do his work. Although most of the other children liked Reese, they complained that he broke the rules when he played games with them. Despite his moments of opposition, Mrs. Leslie liked Reese: He was friendly and seemed to want to please her. Her description of Reese's friendly demeanor was quite at odds with his frowns in my office. Discrepancies like this are not unusual; they remind me and the parents that there is no one "true" setting in which a child's behavior is revealed in all its facets.

I thought about Ari's contention that Reese's behavior was really not so "abnormal for a boy." The expectations for children's school behavior have increased in recent years; at the same time, we've become less comfortable using external rewards and punishments to enforce those expectations. This heaps an extra degree of challenge on boys, who tend to act out under stress or challenge the nearest authority figure; here, the teacher. But the behavior Mrs. Leslie reported—the low-level but frequent interruptions, the rule breaking—was consistent with what I'd seen in the office, and I thought it was fair to ask that Reese conform to higher standards.

I asked Mrs. Leslie how she coped with Reese's problems. She relied mostly on spoken reminders ("Reese, come back to your seat"). Occasionally she would keep him inside during the first few minutes of recess. But none of these strategies seemed to make much difference.

We spent a few minutes talking about the Gardner family situation. She was aware of Holly's difficulties with Reese at home and of disagreements between the parents. "They have such different expectations," she told me with a sigh. Mrs. Leslie noted that Reese was most difficult on Mondays, the day after he made the switch from one parent's home to the other. When we talked about the possibility of psychiatric diagnosis, she acknowledged that although some days were just fine for Reese, his overall behavior reminded her of some other "ADD children." She had passed this impression on to Holly, but she emphasized to me, "I'm not the doctor." I asked if the school had ever performed any educational or psychological testing on Reese; it had not.

I garnered some important information from this fifteen-minute talk. Mrs. Leslie, who came across as a thoughtful person, did indeed perceive some problems with Reese's performance at school; these problems were neither as severe as Holly thought nor as innocuous as Ari believed. Her classroom was of moderate size—twenty kids—which suggested that Mrs. Leslie's observations were not strongly affected by a sense of being overburdened. My suspicion that Reese's problems were aggravated by his parents' tension on transition Sundays was bolstered. I was beginning to feel that a series of behavioral interventions, coordinated among school and both homes, would help Reese, and I felt pretty sure that Mrs. Leslie would be of willing assistance on the classroom front. Regarding medication—well, Reese certainly wasn't so handicapped by his behavior that his schooling was endangered, and Ari's opposition to drugs would have made this therapy difficult to implement in any case. But the fact that Reese's teacher had already taken several reasonable steps to address his problems without success made it slightly more likely that Reese could be a candidate for medication down the road. I still didn't know if Reese had any learning problems that might play into the mix of decisions and interventions.

In addition to speaking with teachers (as well as other educational professionals, such as tutors or coaches), I also feel that it is important to keep the child's primary-care physician in the loop. If medication is eventually prescribed, I will write the first prescriptions and help establish the proper dosing, but the primary-care doctor often writes for the drugs afterward. Like the teacher, the doctor can give me insights that I might not otherwise receive. A statement like "little Audrey has been a real problem since birth" tells me a lot about a child's history and temperament; so do statements like "I've never met the child's father."

When a doctor (or a teacher) disagrees with a parent's perspective, I'm careful not to assume that the doctor is "right" where the parents are "wrong," but a chorus of voices reminds me to stay on my toes.

I spoke briefly with Reese's pediatrician. She told me Reese had no outstanding medical issues and that his vision and hearing had been checked within the year. Reese needed no further physical or laboratory evaluation, nor do the other children who see me unless they have a specific medical problem. There's little value in getting blood tests (unless lead poisoning is of concern), EEGs, or brain scans despite some highly publicized claims to the contrary. His doctor was aware of some of Reese's problems and had considered getting the family some help. She admitted that she was intimidated by the parents' conflict and tried to limit her involvement to issues that were strictly medical. I certainly understood her position and made yet another mental note that any intervention for Reese would require an unprecedented amount of cooperation between Holly and Ari.

Direct Assessment of the Child

At last I was to see Reese alone. After the parent-only and family meetings, I usually meet with any child six or older for about seventy-five minutes. We talk about the problem as well as other matters; if the child is a preadolescent, we also spend some time playing. After this, I screen the child for academic and developmental strengths and weaknesses, using brief age- and grade-based assessment tests. I meet some five-year-olds alone to check on their skills—increasingly necessary, given today's competitive kindergartens.

Some parents are worried that their child won't demonstrate the troublesome behaviors during either the family or the individual visit. It's true that I am often surprised by how much more competent and settled kids are in a one-on-one meeting with me. But this experience doesn't negate reports from home or school. It does point out that there is no single definitive setting for the child. Office and home and school are all important, and none represents the sole reality of a child's life. It is generally a positive sign when a child behaves well in the office. It shows that a child is capable of acting "good," and parents and I can use this knowledge as a factor in treatment. Since I had received such varied accounts of Reese's behavior from the adults in his life, I was curious to see how he'd behave in this particular setting.

Reese followed me into the room where I talk with children by themselves. He was clearly distracted by the shelves of toys along the back wall; I told him that if it was too hard for him to talk we would move back into the more sparsely furnished family room. I got his attention.

Initially he interrupted me as I spoke, just as he did with his father, asking when he could play. However, after about five minutes he settled down and quite competently answered my questions about school and the class rules. Spontaneously he spoke about his parents' continuous battles. He said he told his mom to stop yelling at his father when the parents argued on the telephone. He complained that his father was unfairly holding his Game Boy; Reese couldn't complain to his mother, however, because if she said something it would anger his father and make him keep it longer. He claimed that his father was "stealing" his Game Boy and that he intended to sneak it back into his possession. He told me that he liked his mom more but still liked his dad because they went to baseball games together.

In general, Reese handled our conversation well. Despite the obvious troubles at home, he continued to feel loyalty and affiliation for both his parents. However, when we started to play I noticed some problems. I asked him to tell me a story with the toys, but once again, he couldn't make up his mind. He began with two knights dueling each other but then quickly dropped that in favor of a shark eating a woman on a surfboard, and then he went to yet another scenario. By Reese's age, most kids can develop a narrative without this kind of difficulty. Failure to do so can have any of several causes: disorganization, pervasive anger or other feeling, or developmental delay, among other possibilities.

Reese knocked one of the shelves over and the toys—about seventy-five of them!—slid off onto the floor. As we put the toys back I had to remind him repeatedly that we were cleaning up the toys, not playing with them. This level of opposition and distraction was higher than I usually see in my office; only one other time in ten years has a child knocked over one of my toy shelves. Bear in mind that Reese wasn't in the safety of his home, with parents whose temperaments he knew and of whose love he was assured. He was challenging me—an unknown authority figure, someone who could bite his head off, for all he knew—but he didn't seem to worry much about the consequences. He was much more compelled by the toys. If he acted this way in front of another authority figure, like a teacher, principal, or police officer, he could find himself in serious trouble.

We moved on to thirty minutes of developmental and educational testing. He hopped, skipped, and caught and threw a ball without difficulty. As Mrs. Leslie had noted, he could decode first-grade words, but he had serious trouble understanding a series of disconnected instructions that I read aloud to him. I began to suspect that Reese did indeed have a learning problem, one that hampered his ability to process auditory information. This difficulty, sometimes called a central auditory processing disorder, can be associated with problems in reading comprehension. I didn't feel the problem was severe—more testing was needed to be certain—but I wondered if Reese's difficulty "staying on task" was in part connected to it. If reading or processing the teacher's oral instructions was hard for him, his attention might easily wander to other subjects.

Is It a "Disorder" . . . or a Learning Problem?

Adults go to work and children go to school. In effect, school is a child's job. Melvin Levine, the noted pediatric learning specialist at Duke University, has said that while adults have many endeavors in which to feel successful, children generally have only two: school and sports. Teens also take pride in their social life, especially with the opposite sex.

But learning weaknesses such as dyslexia (difficulty decoding written words) or an auditory processing deficit (problems remembering and using aural information) make school—your child's "career" and source of pride—much more difficult. Some kids may cope with a learning problem by trying harder and drawing on compensatory strengths. But others, like Reese, try to avoid the task, become distracted, or simply refuse to perform. These strategies can look a lot like symptoms of ADHD and ODD. Kids can also experience depression-like symptoms or anxiety, perhaps in the form of stomachaches or obsessive worries about seemingly unrelated things, when their underlying fear is really that "reading is too hard." If parents and professionals are looking too hard for a behavioral "disorder," they can easily miss an underlying learning problem.

I believe that all children with serious behavioral difficulties should be at least screened for learning or processing problems. And kids who have experienced few or no problems at home but get into trouble once they begin school should be checked for a learning disability *before* seeing a therapist or child psychiatrist. I would do the same for kids whose behavior always improves in the summer. There are no drugs that can improve learning problems, but a myriad of classroom strategies as well as specialized pull-out programs are available for kids who have been identified as learning disabled. Although the long-term value of these interventions has never been proven, they unquestionably decrease children's stress and improve their behavior and happiness while they are "at work." A less frustrating experience at school can leave these kids in a better position to take advantage of the more numerous opportunities for success later in life.

After the work, we sat down to a game that I had promised him. We played Crossfire, which involves shooting small pellets from an attached plastic pistol at a sliding target. I was quite clear with Reese about following the rules of the game, threatening to stop play if, for example, he cheated by pushing the target with his hands, as some impulsive children try to do. He managed to play by the rules—yet another positive sign that he could reign in his impulses or aggression—but as I walked out to the waiting room with Reese trailing behind me, he abruptly shut the door and locked it, leaving me standing nonplussed outside.

I felt foolish and a bit annoyed, but mostly I was impressed with Reese's daring and impulsivity. Was he angry with me for winning the game?

I knocked on the door. "Reese, open the door," I said firmly, but without panic or anger.

After a tense moment the door opened with Reese brandishing a broad grin that said, "Gotcha, Dr. Diller!" Before I could say anything, Holly was yelling at Reese for his rudeness. I had an opportunity to regain my composure and appreciate the act.

"Don't do that again, Reese," I said.

"Okay, I'm sorry," he told me, and he seemed to mean it. But I filed away how a similar act in school could have much more serious consequences for him.

Sharing the Findings

After I've met with the parents, the entire family, and the child alone, I like to meet again with just the parents to discuss my observations and feelings. If teenagers are genuinely interested, I include them as well.

As I mentioned in the last chapter, I prefer not to use diagnostic labels like "ADHD" or "oppositional defiant disorder." (An exception occurs when one or both of the parents heavily blame the child or each other. In these cases, a label can take some of the pressure off the "guilty" party and encourage a more productive approach to the problem.) Instead, I describe the child in terms of strengths and weaknesses; I suggest possible causes for the problem and why it continues despite their efforts to help.

I thought long and hard before I decided to ask Reese's parents to come in together for this meeting. I knew from experience that whatever I could do for Reese directly would pale in comparison to the benefits he'd receive if his parents could heal some of their marital wounds and work more closely together. After some negotiation, they both agreed to come in.

When they arrived in my office, they were polite if slightly cool to each other and listened attentively to me. My goal today, I explained, was to help the two of them unite in an approach to help their son, rather than ascribe him to a category and then prescribe medication. "Reese's personality is intense and persistent, with a tendency toward being impulsive. He's basically bright and spunky but often goes too far, like when he locked me out of the office," I told them. "Rather amazing!" I said in mock astonishment. "And when he defied his father with the Lincoln Logs. All of these characteristics make him a challenging kid; no doubt some of your postdivorce problems result from your disagreements about how to handle him. But these traits are exaggerated by your continued fighting and conflicting approaches to parenting. He is testing you, not because he's bad but because he wants to know that you are stronger and more consistent than he is. When you do not set clear limits for Reese and back them up with immediate actions, he pushes even harder.

"In addition, Reese appears to have a learning problem that has not been addressed. This may also make his behavior, especially his inattentiveness, worse. If we get him some help with the learning problem and—most important—if you will cooperate more with each other and agree to try set consistent limits for him, I think we may see some major improvements in his behavior. Let's see what happens if you two and the teacher can get organized. A few months from now, if he's still struggling, I will be more ready to consider medication for Reese."

Ari was pleased that I was not recommending medication at this point, but he was clearly skeptical about working with Holly. For her part, Holly was unsure about forgoing medication, but she expressed hope that she and her ex-husband could coordinate their efforts.

The Follow-Up

Sometimes a complete evaluation includes one or more follow-up sessions. If medication is used, follow-ups are unquestionably necessary, and they need to include enough time for the family's questions about the drug, an examination for side effects, and a discussion of nonmedication approaches that can be used along with the drug. When the child is not using medication, the parents may or may not choose to consult with me further about any behavioral interventions we've discussed. But it can be very useful to discuss how those interventions are proceeding.

In Reese's case, we agreed to meet again. I suggested that when the school year began and Reese started second grade, we set up a time to talk with his new teacher. Holly and Ari seemed both surprised and pleased at my offer to get involved, but in reality it is something I try to do with most of my patients. Often we discuss an individualized educational plan for the child (described in more detail in chapter 6). In Reese's case, I wanted to press for a full psychological and learning evaluation. I also wanted to suggest some ways the teacher could set up a better learning environment for Reese, given his auditory processing problem—she needed to keep her verbal instructions to him short and check to make sure he understood. And I felt that short-term, tangible reinforcements (like stickers and candy for good behavior) and immediate punishments (having to put his head down on the desk) would work better for him than delayed punishments (loss of recess time or a note home).

Holly, Ari, and I discussed how life might be different for Reese in the coming year. Not only would he have a new teacher, he would enter school caught up on his first-grade reading skills. That alone might give him some confidence. And, I hoped, he would have coordinated backup and discipline from both homes, with less tension during the weekly hand-offs. After three months or so into the semester, we would see if he was still struggling. If, despite everyone's best efforts, the problems were still serious, we'd revisit the possibility of using medication during the school day to assist Reese with his impulsivity and work completion. I also recommended that someone—if not me, then another professional—meet with Reese every couple of months to check in with him and see how he was handling the problems between his parents.

Neither parent was entirely satisfied with my suggestions. Ari was especially resistant to the idea of Reese coming in to see me on a regular, even if infrequent, basis. But each of them appeared somewhat pleased that an aspect of their concerns had been acknowledged and reflected in my recommendations. They also seemed relieved, even proud, that they had managed two meetings together without fighting.

"Reese is lucky to have two parents who love him so much. Each of you took a risk by coming here, and I will continue to support your taking those risks to help your son." I meant it. Those of us who are lucky enough to see eye-to-eye with our child's other parent may not realize how difficult it was for Holly and Ari to come together. I doubted that they would ever feel completely comfortable with each other, but for now, even their strained civility would go a long way toward making Reese's life smoother. When they left, I was cautiously optimistic for the three of them. And in fact Reese's behavior did improve over the coming year, to the point that Holly no longer felt he needed medication.

Finding a Practitioner

How do you find someone who practices a complete, ethical evaluation? I suggest that you have a frank conversation with your child's primary-care physician. Explain that you would like a referral to someone who will take *all* the factors of your child's life into account. When you have a name (or, if you're lucky, a list of names), call the evaluator. Ask, What are the steps in your assessment process? Do they include an initial interview, a family interview, time with the child alone, and follow-up meetings? How many of the children in your care take medication? What are some of the nonmedication strategies you employ?

You can also ask family members or trusted friends for referrals, but make sure not to go on blind faith. Pepper the evaluator with the questions listed above. Schools and self-help groups may also offer you names; that's fine, but watch out for a strong biochemical slant.

Throughout this chapter, I've referred to the evaluator as a doctor or a physician—a child psychiatrist, pediatrician (general or behavioral) or a family doctor, anyone who is licensed to prescribe medication. General pediatricians may be useful to parents, since these doctors regularly see healthy, normal children for wellness visits as well as kids with problems. Unlike the other doctors on this list, they are familiar with the wide range of normal behavior and may be less quick to judge a child's actions as "pathological." Such doctors can place your child's problems into perspective and help you determine if you need to seek out further help. However, you may find that many of the doctors in your area (no matter what the specialty) are either enthralled by the biochemical model or handcuffed by insurance companies. Indeed, going to an M.D. these days can be a guarantee that you'll eventually leave with a prescription.

A better first choice may be a psychologist, educational specialist, social worker, or counselor with a specialty in families or children. These professionals may be less focused on the medical model of children's problems and more willing to spend time evaluating and treating their patients. Since they can't prescribe medication, they are generally less hasty to suggest it.

(You should be wary of neo-Freudian therapists who spend week after week in play therapy with a child. Except in cases following trauma, there is no great evidence to support this approach. In my experience, families put too much faith, and lots of money, into prolonged play therapy only to see it fail—and then the child ends up on medication as the apparently sole remaining option.)

I worry when I hear parents paying too much deference to "the doctor" (even when I am the doctor). If parents are too afraid to ask questions or too respectful to state their worries or even their objections, the child is not going to receive the optimum level of help. So make sure that you're comfortable with a practitioner's style and personality. If, after a phone call or even a couple of visits, you feel that the match isn't right, feel free to make a switch. Finally, be on the lookout for "fringe" doctors selling herbs, biofeedback, brain scans, allergy tests, and other dubious diagnostic techniques and therapies. Such strategies may have their uses in other fields (biofeedback can relieve certain painful conditions like headache, for example), but their usefulness for behavioral problems remains unproven. I would also be worried about ADHD specialty clinics. Too often they seem like "mills," churning out one ADHD kid after another on one or two drugs with little follow-up and without other treatment.

A complete, ethical evaluation does not come cheap. If you discover that your favored practitioner does not accept your HMO, you might look into switching to the preferred provider plan (usually called the PPO) on your insurance menu. A PPO is more expensive than an HMO, but you may save money when compared with simply paying out of pocket. If a PPO isn't available or if you don't feel there is time to switch, you need to check your family budget to see if you can afford a thorough evaluation. Each family needs to decide the relative value of a complete and ethical evaluation of their child; obviously, I feel it's worth the cost.

4

When Time-Outs Don't Work: Have You Tried These Strategies for Effective Discipline?

Staff members at the South River Academy, a private school where Ryan Cash attended first grade, were calling his mother with regular complaints. Ryan couldn't focus on his work—he couldn't even stay in his seat. He was constantly interrupting the teacher, leaping up to sharpen his pencil, talking to his table mates, or playing with the classroom computer. The teacher, Mrs. Grey, recommended that Ryan receive a medical evaluation. Since Mrs. Grey had mentioned attention deficit disorder in the past, the Cashes took this statement to mean that Ryan should be tested for ADHD.

Although Susan and Bill Cash were intelligent, careful people, with a master's degree apiece, they were bewildered. They didn't want Ryan to be labeled with a psychiatric disorder, and they were wary of psychiatric drugs. But they thought highly of Ryan's school and of Mrs. Grey in particular and were troubled by her remarks.

I first met Ryan in the company of his parents and his four-year-old sister, Casey. I opened the door between the waiting room and the family meeting room, where a sectional couch faces a loveseat with a solid, low table between them. Both children pushed in ahead of their parents and headed straight for some bins of toys in the far corner.

Ryan found a long rubber snake and began swinging it over his head in an arc.

Susan and Bill sat down on the couch. I reminded the parents that they were in charge of their children's behavior while they were in the office and asked them if they wanted Ryan to continue to swing the snake. "Don't you think you could listen better, Ryan, if you put the snake away?" Susan said. There was no response. Casey had now dug several toys out of the bin and was lining them up on the floor.

Susan tried again. "Okay, kids, it's time for you to put away the toys now." She threw an apologetic glance in my direction and then began to sing a song meant to make cleaning up more fun: "Clean up, clean up, everybody's cleaning up . . . "

The snake whipped through the air. "Ryan," Susan said, her tone changing, "I said to put the snake away." I noted that Bill tended to hang back, deferring to Susan in this matter. "Come on, Ryan," he chimed in a few times.

Finally Susan got up, walked over to Ryan, sat down where he was, and stared him straight in the eye. "Put the snake away *now*," she said. Ryan stopped swinging the snake but did not actually let go of it. Susan placed the remaining toys in the bin and walked Ryan and Casey over to the couch.

Brown-haired, blue-eyed Ryan was a big kid who looked about two years older than his actual age of six. Susan and Bill had told me previously that Ryan's size might have been making things worse for him, since adults tended to ratchet up their expectations based on his height and weight. Some kids would shy away from him, since he could easily knock them over with his physical exuberance. And he was definitely exuberant, with an activity level much higher than that of most kids his age. He was up and down from the couch three times in the first five minutes; even when he was sitting in one place, he was squirming, kicking his legs back and forth, or making circles in the air with his hands and feet. Given the boy's abundant energy, I wondered why the parents didn't have him sitting next to one of them on the couch or even between them, each with an arm around the boy in a lovingly firm embrace. It was early in the evaluation, but I was developing a hypothesis that the Cashes were too passive with their very active son.

I was dubious that I would be able to engage the children, especially Ryan, in a long conversation, so I asked Susan and Bill to perform a short puppet play about a boy who was having some trouble in his classroom. Virtually all children at this age are attracted to stories of power and rule breaking ("It's like Shakespeare to them," I tell parents), probably because issues of security are paramount for them. If Ryan couldn't keep up with his parent's narrative, I would be worried about his abilities. But Ryan settled down—somewhat. When Fred, the puppet child, did not follow the teacher's instructions, Ryan shouted, "Give him a time-out!" His interjection was amusing and demonstrated that he could follow the story and that he knew right from wrong, but he caused several other interruptions during the show. He began to whirl the snake around again, distracting everyone. Although the show was specifically directed to his age and interest level, he was still impulsive enough to wander back to the toy bins (his younger sister sat rapt with attention)—further signs of a problem at a higher level and/or constitutional hyperactivity.

The story ended and I announced a period of free play with the toys. The kids grabbed puppets of their own. I noticed with some consternation that Ryan's efforts were directed at hitting and biting his mother's puppet. It's unusual to see a child so relish hurting and inflicting pain on another, even in play. Susan, with increasing exasperation, valiantly attempted to redirect Ryan's aggressive actions toward something more socially acceptable: "Oh, oh, oh, Ryan. That puppet is being mean." In her puppet's voice, she squeaked, "Can't we be friends? Ooh, he's hurting me. Let's kiss instead." Ryan, with a leer, began biting her puppet's head and making chewing noises with his mouth. He seemed to enjoy his mother's pleading helplessness. Then she took another tack. "Okay, Ryan, if you don't stop being mean with the puppets, Dr. Diller won't let you play with them again." I winced a little to myself. Susan was invoking me as the authority, devaluing herself in the process.

I put out a large sheet of newsprint and asked the family to draw a picture together without talking. The children immediately grabbed markers and began working on their own drawings. The parents did not object, but Susan cleverly added funny hair to Ryan's dog and Bill promptly followed her lead, adding ears to Casey's stick figure. Soon they were all working together. Ryan regularly looked up from drawing at me, as if to say, "Hey, what do you think about how I'm doing?" I got the sense that Ryan was eager for my approval and perhaps not as secure as his bravado suggested.

I recalled how the kids had tumbled into the room ahead of their parents, and they again beat their parents to the punch with the drawing. Both kids were very quick about doing what they wanted and not at all shy about it. Bill and Susan, by contrast, were rather slow with the children. I began to suspect that their temperaments were different from their children's, especially Ryan's. (The hereditary aspects of personality can sometimes skip a generation.) Susan employed a cooperative approach to bringing the children into the family drawing, a creative and certainly very acceptable solution in this case, but not the kind that would work in many situations. Letting the kids charge ahead with the drawing was fine, but if Susan and Bill (as I suspected) set a consistent pattern of allowing the children to lead, how would Ryan or Casey be prepared for times when their parents or schools needed them to follow?

When the Cashes were gone, I was left with the feeling that things were not as easy at home as the parents had suggested in their initial interview with me. A call to Mrs. Grey reinforced my concerns. She had no doubts about Ryan's academic abilities. He was one of her best students in a class of twenty—when he completed his work, that is. But she had to stay on top of him constantly. He pestered the other students so much that none of them wanted to sit next to him.

I inquired about her methods of reinforcing behavior and discipline. The school's policy was to encourage positive behavior with verbal praise. She did not feel comfortable using tangible rewards like stickers; she felt that such rewards encouraged children to work for bribes instead of developing an internal desire to do well. When all else failed, Ryan would be sent to the back of the room for a timeout; on rare occasions, he was taken to the office. I asked Mrs. Grey how much she thought Ryan could control his behavior—what percentage was "can't" and how much was "won't." She said, "Oh, it's virtually all 'can't' in my opinion." She added that while she wasn't a doctor, she'd had "other kids like Ryan who turned out to be ADD."

"Are You Steady and Strong Enough to Take Care of Me?"

Susan and Bill were anxious to hear my thoughts about Ryan. I told them what I honestly felt: that they were loving, caring parents with a basically good family. I acknowledged that many doctors would be ready to diagnose Ryan with ADHD and prescribe Ritalin. Some might diagnose him with oppositional defiant disorder in addition to ADHD. Susan bit her lip at these observations but relaxed when I explained that I preferred to avoid labels for now. Instead, I painted a picture of Ryan as intense, determined, active, and moderately impulsive. Think of Casey, I said. She could certainly test her parents' patience, but she was naturally more compliant—witness how calmly she sat on the couch as we spoke and how engaged she was during the puppet show. Ryan's temperament was different, and it made him more difficult to raise and put through school than other kids. Bill and Susan deserved praise for their obvious devotion and efforts to help him. However, I also felt that his behavior was imbued with additional meaning, a question expressed in his repeated provocations.

"Ryan's problems are a repetitive, unconscious attempt to ask the question: *Are you steady and strong enough to take care of me?* When he misbehaves, you try to help by placating or cajoling him. But Ryan experiences your attempts as weakness. And so he continues to test you, asking you to show that you are steadier and stronger than he is.

"Your goal is a harmonious family and a happy, confident son, which I entirely support. But in this case, because of who Ryan is, the means to your goal cannot be the same as the goal itself. In fact, I'd predict that the more you attempt to achieve this goal with your current method, the further your ideal of harmony and happiness will recede. Are you willing to temporarily put aside your current *means* of working with Ryan and instead respond to his behavior in ways that reassure him of your strength?"

Children need security. They recognize their dependence on you from a very early age; even toddlers understand that they rely on grown-ups to protect them. But kids don't articulate this feeling by saying, "Promise me you'll be stronger than I am." Instead, they test your strength by breaking your rules—they call you names, shove their little sisters, and sneak out of the house. When you respond confidently and with effective consequences, they receive confirmation that you are indeed powerful and consistent enough to guide them safely through life. Kids who experience their parents as strong and steady are more emotionally secure.

But if you fail to set limits, your child experiences himself as more powerful than you are. In the hopes of eliciting a comfortingly potent and steady response from you, the child will test and test again, often escalating the bad behavior—until he gets a satisfying display of authority. (Think of Reese Gardner, who launched his Lincoln Logs about the room over and over until his father finally reacted with a demonstration of force.) This "testing behavior" asks the question: *If I am too little to take care of myself, but I am stronger than you are, then who is taking care of me?*

Isn't Discipline Cruel?

When I first use the word "discipline" (or even worse, the p-word, "punishment") with parents, some of them visibly recoil. (Teachers have a similar reaction.) The word conjures up images of the authoritarian parent, that cold, stiff-jawed figure with a belt at the ready and whose children can never do enough to please. Let me assure you that I am not advocating such an approach. Children absolutely need regular affection. Demonstrations of caring—hugging, kissing, spending time with them on their level—makes them feel loved and validated. ("You'll get more cooperation from a child with whom you just played than if you're always too busy or just want to be left in peace," one parent wisely reflected.) Susan and Bill's strategies of negotiation, offering choices, and reasoning all have their place in good parenting. But for most of the children in my office, love, logic, and choices by themselves have not helped enough. In addition to a warm, loving environment, children need solid discipline to feel secure. Children need both nurturance and discipline; however, both cannot be delivered simultaneously. Trying to do so effectively undercuts one or the other. Discipline is delivered most effectively from a somewhat dispassionate and distanced position.

No one wants to return to the 1930s, when experts favored practices like tying infants' hands to their cribs so they couldn't suck their thumbs, daily enemas from birth to encourage regularity, and avoidance of any physical affection for fear of making children "soft." Most of us today view these methods as nothing less than child abuse. But current popular opinion, which confuses discipline with abuse, is doing us a disservice. Good discipline is not physical harm or emotional injury; it is a kind of teaching or training, one that helps children cope with their inner drives and impulses. In so doing, the child learns to deal with others, comply with rules, and rise to higher standards. The child also develops a much higher degree of confidence.

A Good Fit for Challenging Temperaments

Today's biological psychiatrists, with solid support from the pharmaceutical industry and elements of the disability rights movement, declare that children who are diagnosed with disorders *can't* self-regulate, meaning that the child is incapable of behaving without the aid of drugs. I agree that some kids, like Ryan Cash, have a harder time following rules than others; it's just the way they were born. In Ryan's case, his impulsivity, persistence, and intensity can overwhelm his desire to "be good." In other children, anxiety and obsession can have a similar effect.

But before I medicate a child, I want to know how he will behave if his parents and teachers become more organized and consistent about discipline. In fact, it has been my observation that difficult and sensitive kids need parents who will devote *extra* attention to discipline. These children may need consequences that are especially active and immediate, since their impulses and intensity may make it harder for them to behave the way they'd like. Reasoning, wheedling, and negotiation do not work as well for these kids as the black-and-white choice: Stop misbehaving or life will become unpleasant for you *right now*. (Even adults who have been diagnosed with ADHD say they get along much better when their choices are stark.)

As an exercise of the imagination, compare a challenging disposition with a physical handicap. We would all consider it cruel to ask a child with a shortened leg to walk as fast as someone with two healthy legs. But we would also think it cruel if the parents of that child simply said, "Okay, it's harder for you to walk, so don't even try. I'll carry you wherever you need to go, or you can stay in bed all day." Instead, we rightly feel that it is the parents' job to help the child get about as well as he can. In the same way, challenging kids need extra help from you. They do not benefit from parents who say, "You can't help yourself because you have a chemical imbalance. Therefore, I will not expect much from you." They deserve compassion and understanding, but they also need discipline that they will comprehend and to which they will respond.

CHECK YOUR OXYGEN MASK

When flight attendants instruct passengers on the use of emergency equipment, they give special instructions to those traveling with a young child: "First, place the mask over your face; then place a mask over the child's." Otherwise, both parent and child may pass out.

Too many parents don't have enough oxygen flowing in their daily lives. Parents who are overworked or depressed, are in a miserable marriage, or abuse drugs/alcohol cannot be a source of strength and consistency for their children. After all, if you can hardly catch a breath, how you will find time or energy to follow through on your rules? Overtaxed parents often ignore their children's testing behaviors; when pushed to their limits, they react by screaming or insulting or even hurting the child. If you are suffering from a significant emotional, marital, or substance-abuse problem, you *must* address it before you can tackle discipline.

The stress of raising a temperamentally challenging child can itself cut off your air supply. When a parent seems really beaten down or depressed, we might begin by assisting the flow of oxygen, perhaps in the form of self-care (getting some exercise, having a kid-free lunch out with friends) or even medication for the parent. This is not a way of blaming the adult but simply an acknowledgment that parents must be able to breathe before they can be effective. Sometimes, when I see parents in trouble—let's take marital problems as an example—I strike a bargain with them: "Let's see if you two can work together on the consistency and discipline stuff." (The marriage may even improve if the couple can achieve some success together with the children's problems.) "If so, we'll defer the other issues. But if your differences over money and sex make it too difficult for you guys to trust each other or work together on discipline, then we'll have to focus on those other problems."

Single parents are particularly susceptible to oxygen depletion. Even those who are exceptionally competent may burn out when dealing with a difficult child, recalcitrant school system, or demanding boss. Single parents face the additional heavy burden of having to make all the important decisions about their kids *by themselves*. Several single parents meet with me once or twice annually simply to use me as a sounding board for their judgments about their children.

Although I'm certain there are some truly irresponsible single parents—just as there are some truly irresponsible married ones—few make it to my office. More commonly, the single parents I see shoulder heavy feelings of guilt and responsibility for their family's plight, which binds them tightly to a 24/7 service for their kids. I try to convince them that if they want to be more effective with their kids, they need to take some time just for themselves, perhaps to read a good novel, catch a movie, or unwind with friends. However, I also recognize that freeing up time, energy, and money for these breaks may itself be a Herculean task for the single parent.

Taking Effective Action

Effective discipline is not easy to achieve with difficult and persistent children. ("I'd do anything for my kid," one father told me. "So why is it so hard to say no?") Most parents come to me only after time-outs, scolding, yelling, and even spanking have failed. This was the case with Susan and Bill Cash. When Susan's attempts at pleading with Ryan went unheeded, she sometimes became so angry that she screamed at him. He would be frightened and comply, but afterward she felt horribly guilty, vowing never to raise her voice again. They had given up on time-outs because Ryan would either run out of his room (their designated time-out location) or howl and wail as if he were being tortured.

However, both Susan and Bill appreciated my proposition. Apparently, Susan—on whose shoulders most of the disciplinary decisions rested—had already been thinking a great deal about their parenting style. She herself had been raised more strictly and judged her childhood as positive. Her current techniques of pleading and placating, she said, left her discontented. But she had received so much contradictory advice from the school, her pediatrician, and myriad parenting books that she felt paralyzed. She wanted the children to have freedom to express themselves; that's why she let them take the lead during the drawing exercise and many other family activities. She did not want to limit their choices. But it also made sense to her that children needed preparation following rules at home if they were to succeed in other settings. Bill, who was by nature a pretty laid-back guy, was also willing to make a change. He indicated that he was willing to become more involved in house discipline than he had been before.

One of Susan and Bill's most noticeable problems was that Ryan ignored their spoken commands. He'd learned that their verbal requests held few unpleasant consequences for him, so he simply stopped listening. I felt that Susan and Bill could restore power to their words by taking action after only one or two verbal warnings.

"What kind of action?" Bill asked. I've noticed that even the most passive parents resort to some kind of action when the child repeatedly provokes them and makes them really angry. Susan told me that she tended to scream; Bill found himself engaged in those howling, furious time-outs. Another good example is Ari Gardner. When Reese's behavior started getting questionable, Ari would use gentle spoken reminders, which his son blissfully ignored. Reese's behavior grew wilder and wilder, until Ari went over the edge. Then Ari would sweep away his toys or bark at him, and Reese would stop.

Each of these parental actions was ultimately unsatisfying. By the time the parents took action, emotions on all sides had escalated; the increased level of intensity between the parents and child made the battle more difficult and unpleasant. I am also concerned when parents act only when borne along a tidal wave of anger or frustration, because a parent who is out of control will often truly frighten a child. Parents who wait for anger to dissolve their ambivalence about "being mean" are strapping their children aboard a roller-coaster ride of permissiveness and discipline—hardly conditions that satisfy a child's need for security.

What I usually tell parents is this: *Take the same action you would take if you were angry; just do it sooner.* For Susan, that might mean throwing a sharp but controlled tone into her voice; Bill could conduct a time-out before Ryan's emotions had completely overwhelmed both of them. Ari could calmly but decisively remove Reese's toys after one or two reminders and then withhold them for a few minutes.

No matter what the action, it must occur quickly. If your child is five or younger, you need to respond within seconds. For five- to ten-year-olds, the consequences can occur minutes later. Kids eleven and older can handle delayed consequences, but it's still best to have them happen on the same day. And kids who are impulsive, no matter what their age, will generally need action sooner rather than later. Their temperament makes it harder for them to care about a threatened punishment that's anything other than immediate.

I asked Susan and Bill to target one or more regularly recurring problems with Ryan, problems that would allow them to respond with a specific, prompt action. They decided to work on having Ryan sit for five minutes at the dinner table and on getting ready for school in the morning without so much fussing and delay.

At dinner, they would use a timer to help Ryan monitor himself. They were prepared to let him miss his meal altogether (without sneaking him any snacks later in the night) if he failed to sit. If he remained in his seat for the five minutes, he would get an extra helping of dessert.

We also altered the morning routine. "There is a new rule in this house," Susan and Bill announced to Ryan. "In the morning, you must get out of bed, eat breakfast, brush your teeth, and comb your hair before you are allowed to put on your school clothes." They would give him three reminders before seven o'clock, when the family had to leave, so that he'd know how much time was remaining. Whether he dawdled or delayed was his choice, but any clothes not on him by seven o'clock would be put in a shopping bag left near the front door. He would be taken into school in his pajamas and would have to get dressed there. (I told the parents to actually let him get dressed in the backseat of their car on the first transgression, but not to tell him about this partial amnesty in advance. Although I felt that the chances were slim that Ryan would fail to cooperate, we also alerted Mrs. Grey to their plan.) If Ryan became angry as his parents enacted the new rules for dinner or the morning, both Susan and Bill were prepared to take him to a time-out.

The Effective Time-Out

Time-outs are the socially approved method of handling anger over rules. They're also used for raucous or severe misbehavior, like throwing a tantrum or striking out at a parent or another child. Some parents use them for lesser offenses, like simple but clear disrespect—say, responding with a bronx cheer when a firm "no" is delivered. Since both Susan and Bill liked the basic premise of a time-out but had encountered difficulty making it work, we went over the procedure in the office.

The time-out technique can be blessedly simple. When a bottom line is crossed, the parents start to count: one . . . two . . . three. If the behavior has not stopped by the count of three, the child is given a time-out, which means being taken (or sent) to a nonstimulating location, such as a chair in a far corner or a quiet room. During a time-out, a child may be permitted a limited expression of anger, but not hitting, kicking, or destructive behavior.

Sounds easy enough in theory, but problems like the Cashes experienced are common and can be discouraging. Some kids refuse to go to or stay in time-out. Other children thrash their arms and legs around, making them difficult if not dangerous to handle. There are those who pull apart their rooms; I've even known kids to climb up on a ledge and shout out the window to the neighborhood (usually something about the unjustness of their parents!). Another extreme is kids who "go Gandhi," letting their bodies fall limp and making it hard to get the child to time-out. Susan and Bill found that Ryan yelled and sometimes refused to stay in his time-out spot.

We agreed that they might have more luck with time-outs if they took action earlier, before emotions escalated on both sides. If they could move more quickly, with a serious but controlled intensity, it was possible that Ryan would not be so wild and crazy and that he would obey faster. I asked Susan and Bill if they were willing to endure some dramatic noises, like his howling. And if he didn't honor the rules of time-out, I asked them, would they be willing to show him that they were still stronger than he? I suggested they adopt one of three methods: a quick spank to his thigh or bottom, returning him to his room or bed with a firm shake, or holding him in place. I noted that most parents do not have any qualms about using physical restraint under certain circumstances, such as when a child is about to run out into the street. Bill and Susan saw the connection and agreed that they would try.

Whether to use physical discipline remains a personal choice for parents, but I don't think it is damaging or dangerous if a parent of a child aged two to nine or ten occasionally decides to spank the child or to sit him down firmly on a bed or chair in the service of maintaining a time-out. Some parents prefer the more passive method of holding a kicking, screaming child in place by grasping his arms and legs. That is another personal choice and one that can work quite well—I sometimes show parents a wrap-around holding technique that minimizes thrashes and escapes. But parents should not be under any illusions. Holding down an actively resisting child is often more difficult and more uncomfortable, even painful, for both the parent and child than a swat on the bottom or thigh. (When parents do not wish to use force but are faced with a child who fights time-out, they might consider extending the time-out period or adding an additional consequence for misbehavior. I've found that these responses take much longer to work and are less effective, but parents must discover what works best for them.)

I reminded Susan and Bill not to undertake any physical elements of a time-out when they felt themselves becoming overwhelmed with anger. Most parents who see me are able to easily navigate the line between discipline that has a physical component and injury or abuse. But it is wise to remember that this line can sometimes be crossed. I've occasionally seen parents employ time-outs in a way that made me uncomfortable. Once I witnessed a father attempt to put his fifteen-year-old son into a time-out in my office. Before I could stop them, Charley, the father, grabbed Jason, the boy, by the arms and tried to shove him into the corner. Jason refused to go, and his father pushed him. At this point, I was very worried. Charley was a big man—about 240 pounds. Although Jason was probably a hundred pounds lighter, he had the advantage of being fueled by teenage embarrassment and anger. They were closely enough matched for someone to get hurt. So I stood up and ordered Charley to back off. He did, and Jason remained where he was, both of them breathing heavily.

When we spoke later, Charley reminded me that I had given him permission to get physical with Jason in order to maintain a time-out. "That's right, Charley," I said. "But I gave you that advice six years ago, when Jason was nine. Now that he's bigger, you can't conduct time-outs in the same way. It's too dangerous."

I recommended that Susan and Bill use a physical response no more than twice per episode. More than that, and parents can get overheated. I told them, "If you rely on force twice and still don't see success, you can say, 'Okay, Ryan, you won this time. But next time, I'm prepared to do the same thing again.' Ryan may seem thrilled with his 'triumph,' but in fact he hasn't liked the experience at all. The knowledge that you're not going to shy away the next time really gets to him. Parents don't have to 'win' every time, but when they stay consistent, the kid will learn that you are indeed more determined, more assured, and more able to provide him with the security he needs to handle his emotions and behavior."

Susan volunteered that when she had tried time-outs, she felt sorry for Ryan and stretched out the count: "Ryan, that's one. Ryan, that's two. Ryan, that's two. Did you hear me? That's two." She came to her own conclusion that this probably gave Ryan the message that she was unwilling to take him to the time-out; I would add that it tends to escalate the conflict. It's also ineffective. (One day, I was entering the post office when I saw a mother trying to cajole her four-year-old son out of the bushes. "Simon, come out of there right now," she said. "I'm counting! One . . . two . . . two . . . two . . . two . . ." I stood in line at the counter, mailed my package, and left the building before Simon came out.)

If you would like to learn more about time-outs, I highly recommend Tom Phelan's book *1-2-3 Magic*. It's a short, quick read and is also available on video. The book and video first describe the time-out technique and then give examples of how children ages two to twelve try to knock parents off course, with suggestions for standing firm.

Talk Less and Be Heard

Susan and Bill returned the next week, pleased and astonished at Ryan's improvements in the mornings and at dinner. As I had expected, he responded quickly to the new morning schedule. Susan noted that it required restraint on her part to give Ryan only three warnings and to keep quiet in between, but she agreed that limiting her words made them much more ominous and effective. (Some parents express wariness over this method, concerned that their child would be humiliated by being pulled half-dressed into school. I have known very few kids to test their parents even once when this routine and its consequences are articulated. I also believe that a briefly unhappy experience of showing up once at school in pajamas, if it subsequently changes morning behavior, is better for the child than years of arguments over school preparation.)

Dinner was more of a struggle, but Ryan made it through the five-minute period most nights. The third evening, Ryan aggressively pushed back his chair from the table before the timer went off and zoomed toward the television. "This is your warning. Come back or it's time out," Susan said to him. Ryan turned on his heel and stalked down the hall. Susan was prepared for this response and felt sure of herself, she told me. Bill reported that since Susan had initiated the warning he would let her follow through with action. However, they had agreed ahead of time that whichever parent was inactive would keep an eye on the other. (My wife and I have a code phrase, "Atlantic Ocean," for such situations. We use it when one of us has been wheedling with the kids for too long without taking action, but it can also be used to gently warn a parent who is working up too much lather. The idea behind a code word or phrase is that the active parent isn't visibly undermined by the other in front of the kid.)

Susan jumped up from her chair and caught up with Ryan, grabbing him by the arm. "You're going to time-out now," she told him. "Ouch! Ouch! You're hurting me!" Ryan yelled. Susan glimpsed down at Ryan's arm; she was holding him tightly but was not injuring him. "Right!" she said back. "That's the point, buddy." Ryan looked surprised but stopped protesting. She escorted him into his room and sat him down firmly on his bed. She waited, ready for him to get up and try to run out, but he stayed put.

The next night, Ryan sat through the five minutes without complaint and even contributed a couple of anecdotes from school. He was regularly getting his extra dessert, which, in addition to the praise of both his parents, made him happy. (By the way, Susan and Bill applied these same rules to Casey too. She did some testing of her own but in general went along with the new restrictions more easily than her brother did.)

During later meetings, I noticed a change in Susan's words and tone of voice. Gone were the questions like "Do you want to help clean up the toys?" Instead, with her voice deepening just a bit and her tone lowering at the end, she'd say, "Help me clean up the toys now." For his part, Bill was visibly willing to participate in a solid, methodical approach—as it turned out, that support was all Susan really needed.

Susan ventured her surprise at how well both her children now responded to her verbal reminders. I wasn't surprised. Not only was her tone more businesslike, Ryan and Casey had learned to associate their parents' requests with quick action. It's just one of the many ironies of parenting that when you talk less, your kids hear you more clearly. (When I asked a seven-year-old girl if things had improved at her house after her parents began a system of limits and consequences, she nodded and said, "Mom's mouth isn't as tired anymore.")

Reward Systems

Ryan's behavior also improved at school. I called Mrs. Grey and explained that I felt Ryan's personality would make it harder for him to respond to rewards and punishments that depended on cognition and delay. I mentioned that his parents were having some success with immediate, tangible rewards, like dessert when Ryan stayed at the table. Mrs. Grey listened with interest and decided she was open to a new tactic. At my suggestion, she presented Ryan with a "star opportunity" twice a day, usually about ten or twenty minutes before a fun activity like recess, lunch, computer time, or an art project. Ryan would be given a specific amount of work to accomplish in a reasonable amount of time. If he completed the work, he would receive a star sticker affixed to a card that was sent home with him every day to his parents. The stars were convertible at the end of the week for prizes or privileges. If he received ten stars, Ryan could choose the book the teacher would read aloud on Fridays. If he amassed twenty, he could choose from a selection of small toys. (Sometimes parents provide these rewards at home, but Mrs. Grey decided to offer them to Ryan herself.)

But there was another side to the star opportunity: If Ryan did not perform a minimum amount of assigned work, or if he required more than one reminder to stick with the task, the star would be withheld *and* he would remain behind the rest of the class for five minutes as they engaged in the upcoming activity. (There was no need for him to miss *all* of recess or other forms of fun; five minutes of waiting while the other kids play is agony enough for any young child.) She found that giving immediate rewards worked so well with Ryan that soon she was offering stars to the entire class.

I didn't worry that Ryan would become dependent on the stars or on the extra helping of dessert in order to meet basic expectations; all practical and research evidence contradicts this belief. Study after study shows that rewards can eventually be delayed or used intermittently once good habits are in place and then eventually removed. In fact, all of us work for rewards; it's just that some of us are better at delaying our gratification (doing homework all semester in the hopes of a good report card or working hard at the office for a promotion) or have internalized the reward (perhaps pride in a job well done). Some children, especially those with difficult or sensitive temperaments, may need a more immediate, concrete reward system for a while, just as they often require an immediate consequence for misbehavior. Not to mention that most kids who are Ryan's age think that it's fun to work for rewards like coins or stickers or stars.

SETTING LIMITS FOR ADOLESCENTS

If you make rules and enforce them for your sixteen-year-old the same way you did when he was four, you're likely to have a major rebellion on your hands, one that's supported by popular culture and the teen's peers. And, as the story of Jason and Charley demonstrates, it's simply too dangerous for parents of teens to employ a physical bottom line.

But teens still need (and appreciate) rules and limits. Broader parameters that respect the child's growing maturity are usually best. Checking homework every night to see that it's done is likely to be resented as overly controlling by the teen. A more useful strategy may be to inform the child that how he gets his homework done is up to him; but you will be receiving a progress report from his teachers at the end of the week, and if there are any in-complete assignments, there will be no phone privileges for the weekend.

Teens are more capable than smaller children of using time-de-layed consequences. They don't necessarily need rewards or pun-ishments to occur within seconds, although you may find that your teen responds better to consequences that occur on the same day or, at most, in the same week. You can also use your teen's ability to think more rationally than a young child—with the caveat that teens are more capable of logic when it doesn't apply to them! Discussing problems with them can sometimes elicit their cooperation. It's cer-tainly worth a try. And when you and your teen disagree, the simple act of listening to the teen's point of view and acknowledging it may go far in tempering any anger or disappointment over your decision.

In the end, though, the teen has to *want* on some level to con-trol himself, either for his own reasons or because he doesn't want to hurt his parents' feelings too much. If a teen is intent on break-ing rules and challenging authority, it will be very tough for the parent to sufficiently monitor and protect the child. Keeping the kid and others safe may become a primary concern and difficult to do at home. Some families have success in sending their teen to a controlled environment, like a special boarding school or Outward Bound-type program.

Most out-of-control teens are not ready to use a therapist in order to make a change, and a doctor alone can't provide the mo-tive for improvement. But a professional can still offer regular sup-port and can help make sure the teen isn't into something too self-destructive. When the teen *does* begin to question what he's doing to himself (some will need to hit rock-bottom first; others may take stock as they grow older), an established relationship with a thera-pist can help the teen organize his thoughts and work on his actions.

I also suggest that the parents of these teens seek professional support. Living with these kids is like being on a roller-coaster ride; look for a therapist who can help you anticipate the next curve. Having someone to talk to can make the journey a little less frightening and lonely.

A "Proven Parenting Method"?

Within a couple of weeks, I saw a difference in both Ryan's and Casey's level of activity in my office. I think they, like other kids I have seen, relax when they don't feel the need to test their parents so often. Of course, both children still needed warnings from their parents and also time-outs—no kid is an angel, and you don't change five years of previous behavior in two weeks. Other aspects of Ryan's life took longer to address. It was several months before his unhappy, aggressive play began to shift. Susan and Bill would warn him when his actions got out of line, and the family and I played board games as part of our meetings. (I like games not as therapy per se but because they reflect the real-life problems of having to take turns, win or lose graciously, and obey rules, among other things.) Ryan's eventual long-term improvement, I felt, was a result of being in a new pattern of behavior. He felt secure with his parents and confident that he was performing well at home and school; he no longer felt, in his own judgment, that he was "bad."

Ryan's experience is unusual in my practice only in that I believed the impulsive aspects of his personality were quite strong. I was genuinely prepared to offer him Ritalin if the efforts of his parents and school failed to help him sufficiently. But as it turned out, Ryan, like so many impulsive, defiant, sad, anxious, or obsessive children, succeeded when his caregivers made specific changes in their behavior toward him.

However, the Cash family's success was not dependent on any one technique we discussed in my office. The time-out, the clothes in the bag, the timer at dinner—none of these strategies means much in and of itself. There's no such thing as a "proven parenting method" that, once learned by all parents and universally set into motion, will assist every child. What made the difference for Susan and Bill was the new level of confidence they brought to their endeavor. It helped them to have a plan in mind, but the plan worked only because Susan and Bill had resolved their ambivalence about discipline. They presented their case to Ryan with authority and were willing to follow through. It was this attitude, more than anything else, that helped Ryan feel safe and secure enough to cut back on his testing behaviors.

Other parents have found it liberating to discover that it's okay to ask their child to live up to reasonable standards. One father confessed to me, "Once you told me my little girl doesn't have ADHD, that she's just intense and persistent, I felt I could expect more from her behavior." The girl's mother had a different—actually, a nearly opposite—reaction to the same words I'd used to describe their child, yet she still felt more comfortable about taking control. She said, "Now I know that it's much harder for her to regulate her emotions and behavior without help from us." They both felt less guilty about providing some additional external control in the form of effective limits, and their daughter improved rapidly in the face of their newfound authority.

How do you develop this kind of confidence? I am reminded of Susan's dilemma: The heaps of advice from authors and doctors had a paradoxical immobilizing effect, so that she minutely scrutinized every parenting decision and quashed her own sensible ideas. With that in mind, I say to you: I have seen thousands of children improve with limits and discipline. But there is no single approach that works all the time for all children or all parents. Your individual style and your knowledge of your child must be brought to bear as you conduct the long trial-and-error process that is parenting. Despite my emphasis on setting limits, I know from clinical as well as personal experience that on occasion, the most useful thing parents can do with their wailing, whining six-year-olds is not to discipline them but to hold them close and whisper sweet nothings into their ears.

Parenting temperamentally challenging children is like playing an antique violin. Bow too softly and you hear nothing. Bow too hard and it squeaks. Finding just the right amount of pressure to make the difficult but beloved instrument sing sweetly requires much skill and practice. Counsel with an expert, called behavioral management training, and advice from a book can help you with technique, but ultimately you must play the instrument yourself.

5

Beating Mrs. Bossy and Defeating Darth Vader: Can You Externalize the Problem?

Eight-year-old Timmy's hands were red and chapped, the result of washing them nearly twenty times a day. He was afraid of giving germs to his playmates; if his friends died, Timmy said, he might be arrested. He refused to roughhouse with other kids, go to parties, or even visit other kids' houses. At home, he would tremble if for some reason he couldn't wash his hands as soon as he felt the need.

So far, Timmy's teacher had been understanding, but she was concerned that Timmy's frequent need for hand-washing trips was causing him to miss classroom time. Timmy's mother was more alarmed. "What happens when you die?" he asked her. "How do germs kill you?" After she discovered uneaten sandwiches in his backpack, Timmy confessed: He would no longer eat in the "dirty" school cafeteria.

Regina, Timmy's mother, a medium-built woman with short, sandy hair, explained all of this in my office. She leaned forward in her chair with some pain and intensity in her voice. She told me that she and her husband had reassured Timmy endlessly that germs weren't going to kill him or his friends. They tried to be compassionate, going out of their way to help Timmy avoid distressing circumstances. They would pick up toys that he was afraid to touch, and they allowed him to leave the dinner table early and avoid Sunday school. "On top of everything else, he's beginning to feel guilty about all the soap he's using," she sighed, clearly frightened and frustrated that her little boy was losing this battle with his irrational thoughts. "The psychologist we took Timmy to said he had obsessive-compulsive disorder and should take medication."

I wasn't against using medication to help Timmy. Regina's description of Timmy's behavior certainly met most doctors' criteria for the obsessive-compulsive disorder (OCD) diagnosis, and I found the degree of his troubles worrying. I was even more daunted by the family's history of psychiatric problems: Four members of Timmy's immediate family, including both of his parents, were currently taking psychoactive drugs. More than anything, I worried that the family's previous commitment to psychiatric medication would make them skeptical of any alternative proposal. Studies have shown that the single greatest influence on the decision to medicate a child is whether one or both parents take a psychiatric drug.

But I thought Timmy would be better off in the long term if he and his family learned to deal with his personality and cope better with life rather than depend on medication. And my Hippocratic oath as a physician, "First do no harm," steered me away from exposing Timmy to the unknown risks of taking a Prozac-type drug (none of these medications has been studied for long-term efficacy or side effects on children), at least before we tried a nondrug approach that has been effective for kids with similar troubles.

Meet Sneaky Poo

In the late 1980s, a fresh voice on the family therapy scene was heard from an unfamiliar source: Adelaide, Australia. Michael White, a family therapist who practiced there, articulated a clever approach to addressing psychological problems. He called it *externalization*.

I clearly remember the first time I heard him speak. I was at a conference, and he was talking about how externalization had helped a young boy suffering from encopresis, the medical term for fecal soiling. White helped the boy reframe his problem as an entity that existed apart from the child. It was a dastardly, sneaking enemy, White suggested, who was wrecking the life of this child and his family. Together, he and the boy gave the enemy a name: Sneaky Poo! He proposed to the child that they form a team and devise ways to defeat this terrible menace. The boy was delighted and agreed to some sensible measures to fight Sneaky Poo, including the regular dietary and bowel habits that he had been avoiding or forgetting. This construction of the problem as external—outside of the child and not an intrinsic part of his makeup— had great appeal not only to the child and his parents but also to the large audience of therapists attending the conference with me.

Much of what White proposed is part and parcel of a cognitive-behavioral approach to therapy, which suggests that if you can get people to name and recognize their maladaptive patterns, you can encourage them to think and act differently. In fact, I had been doing something similar, which I called "combating the problem," for years. But White's formulation offered a higher level of drama and narrative. His concrete, deliciously evil characters (never the children themselves) and combat aspects thoroughly engaged the children, as well as adults in their lives. My particular variation on White's work has been to shift the main arena of the child's externalized problem to the realm of the *parents'* ideas and action. What can they do to help their child recognize and defeat Sneaky Poo (or Darth Vader or Mrs. Bossy or The Pits—whatever name the child wishes to give the problem)? I find that when the parents are highly involved, rapid change can take place.

Timmy Versus the Bully

I attempted to plant a seed of doubt about the inevitability of drugs for Timmy and see how Regina would respond: "You know, I've had some pretty good success helping kids like Timmy without using medication. I'm wondering how you'd feel if Timmy could improve without taking a drug?" Of course, I had loaded the question. What parent wouldn't want their child to improve—and if it could be done without medication, so much the better? Yet given Timmy's family history, I would not have been surprised if Regina had simply said that she thought it very unlikely and wanted her son to have immediate relief—in other words, a drug.

But Regina turned out to be an optimist. She sat up straighter and seemed more alert. "If you think you can help Timmy without using medication, that would be great." Like many parents, what she most wanted was a *plan*. We set up an appointment for me to meet Timmy and another for him with both his parents. The week after, I wanted to meet the whole family. Regina agreed.

When Timmy and Regina arrived for their appointment, I was happily surprised that he separated easily from his mother, who remained in the waiting room. He was a fair-haired, blue-eyed child, a slight boy whose size contrasted with his deliberate, intelligent conversation. "I think about germs a lot—constantly," he said grimly. "Germs can make the other people sick."

Timmy agreed that talking about his problems with his parents or the psychologist hadn't really helped, yet he continued to do so because he was worried. He didn't like washing his hands so much or missing his lunch, but he didn't want to contaminate his friends. Although he listened when his parents and teacher tried to reassure him, he was not convinced.

Unlike some children, who appear to recite what their parents have said to them or are simply unfocused, Timmy spoke steadily and forthrightly, much like a child who was in physical pain and was trying to help the doctor by supplying the information requested. He didn't cry or whine. His intensity confirmed the seriousness of his problem and the unusual degree of his misery.

Unlike many other doctors, I wasn't interested in learning much more about the content of his worries. I didn't think it would do much good.

Nor did I think that my reassuring him or putting his worries in per-spective would be helpful. Other important people in his life had already tried that approach unsuccessfully, and I had no reason to think that I would be an exception. Instead, I began to ask him about variations in the intensity of his worries and moments when the worries were not as great, a process some have called "solution-oriented therapy." Seeking out exceptions to problem behavior can give parents and children a much-needed boost of hope and confidence. When they realize the problem isn't *always* there, it seems much less monolithic, less a matter out of their own control. It can also point to strategies for the future. (For example, the parents of an acting-out child may discover that she actually behaves well rather frequently but that certain circumstances—say, quietly returning to class after an unstructured, freewheeling re-cess—trigger problems. If the child does better when an adult has orga-nized a game during recess, then the parents and school may have some success in keeping things more structured for her during "free" play.)

We quickly made up a list of situations in which the worries were stronger or weaker, greater or smaller. Timmy agreed that when he was concentrating on other things, especially at school, the worries both-ered him less. When he was playing with his friends, or when he was in a good mood in general, "the bad thoughts weren't there," as he put it.

Conversely, if he finished his work at school and was reading a book, the worries would come back. If he was alone, as opposed to being with friends, or if he was angry instead of happy, "the thoughts don't go away." I prompted some of these variations with my knowledge of what other kids have told me, but he strongly agreed with my guesses.

Then I asked him if he had ever gotten over any other fear—again, looking for an example of competence and a source of hope. He said he didn't know. "I know one," I confidently stated. I proposed he was probably scared at one point about riding a two-wheeled bicycle, but not anymore. But I learned I was wrong and felt foolish. Timmy said he was still too afraid to try a two-wheeler, even though he wanted to ride with his friends. So I quickly backtracked. "Well, I know one *for sure*," I said, sounding like a chastised, stupid grown-up. "Yeah, what?" he said, intrigued. "Well, when you first started to learn to walk, do you think you were worried about falling down?" He smiled and nodded his head yes. "And are you worried when you walk now?" He smiled again and said no.

"And how do you think you learned to walk and stop worrying about falling?" I asked, but this time I didn't wait for his answer. "You had courage. You really wanted to walk and you tried and tried and were successful. After a while you became so good at it that you stopped even being concerned about falling down. Am I right?" He said yes. "Well, okay. This worrying problem has got you all bossed around right now, and we've got to find a way that *you* can become more of the boss of the problem. But there's only one way to get over your worries, and that is to have the courage to face them. Do you understand?" He agreed and was with me, smiling and laughing quietly as I talked.

He then remembered that he used to be afraid of the family car crashing and that he was initially afraid to sleep in a bed rather than his crib (he didn't make the change until age four). I congratulated him on his previous victories over fear. Having beaten it before, he could do it again. But I reassured him that we wouldn't try to tackle the most difficult worries first. I helped him construct an anxiety thermometer—an idea I borrowed from John March, a child psychiatrist at Duke University, who came up with a thermometer that measures levels of worry instead of heat. At the 98.6 degree mark, we wrote down two items that he used to be afraid of but was no longer: sleeping in a bed and walking. I asked him what would be the hardest thing to do given his fear of germs. "Rolling around in the mud getting dirty with my friends," he said with a slight smile. We assigned a temperature of 104 degrees to mud rolling.

We then categorized in varying degrees other activities that were less difficult than the mud roll, like eating his lunch at school or touching objects around his house. We assigned them a temperature of 100 degrees. I said that after we met with his mom and dad we might begin taking on one of these items. But right now, I wanted him to think of a name for the problems that this anxiety was creating for him.

Timmy came up with "the Bully." We agreed that the Bully wasn't a real person but a set of ideas and feelings that was bossing Timmy around too much. Our job was to form a team that included his parents and teacher, a team that would help him get the Bully off his back—to put Timmy more in control of his thoughts instead of allowing his thoughts to control him. I'm not sure how much Timmy actually understood, but he seemed excited and positive as we brought his mother in to explain our conversation to her. She too smiled when we told her about the variations in his worrying, previous episodes of overcoming a fear (she added two more that she remembered), the need for courage, the anxiety thermometer, and beating the Bully. I felt encouraged by their response but still wanted to wait until I met Timmy's father to try anything. My experience told me that his position might make or break the treatment.

Bill, Regina, and Timmy came two days later, in my last hour of the day, the only slot Bill's work schedule would allow. Bill was a middle-aged man with a lugubrious air about him. He sighed frequently and spoke in a voice that at times approached a whisper. He seemed terribly burdened by his son's problem, and he also said quite clearly at the outset that he thought Timmy had a disorder, just as he did. He believed that Timmy had inherited his traits of anxiety and panic. Bill recalled that he too began experiencing worries around age eight and thought that Timmy would benefit from a medication.

I felt the power and pressure of this man's resignation toward his son's fate and privately wondered if he would walk away if Timmy did not receive a drug. Again, I considered medicating Timmy immediately, if only to keep his family involved in therapy.

But I decided to press just a bit more. I told Bill that I was certain that biological processes were involved in Timmy's behavior; however, just as in adult-onset diabetes or hypertension, often the first interventions—weight loss, exercise, stress reduction—are environmental. I explained that Timmy's level of worry was *not* steady; sometimes he was completely free of his anxiety. Aloud, I wondered if we could somehow increase his worry-free time.

I brought both Timmy and Regina into the conversation. Timmy was delightfully matter-of-fact with his father over the anxiety thermometer and naming the problem the Bully. Regina's optimism came through as well, and Bill, to my surprise, said, "Okay, let's see what happens without drugs." I was pleased, but now I *really* felt the pressure to get something going. I knew that although initial suggestions from the doctor are critical in guiding the family toward success, it was ultimately up to Timmy and his parents to beat the Bully.

We looked at the anxiety thermometer and decided that eating lunch at school in some limited way might be achievable for Timmy. Regina offered to give him wipes to clean his hands and the table before he ate. I reminded Timmy that he would need courage to take on the Bully, who was trying to make him afraid. Timmy said he wanted to try.

I met Timmy's whole family, including his brothers and sisters, at the next visit. They formed a friendly, caring group. I sensed they were protecting one another's feelings, as if there might be secrets among them. In this setting, Bill emerged as the family patriarch. Although he did not say much, family members tended to hang on his every word. Even his rate of breathing or sighing made a difference in their words and behavior. I sensed that they knew he was deeply hurting but did not dare speak openly about it. I filed these observations away for future reference.

Meeting the parents alone a couple of days later, I wanted to review in detail my thoughts about Timmy's problems and some strategies to help him with the Bully. I found they had already made some progress: Timmy was now eating some, although not all, of his lunch at school. I told them he would need special inducements to try to beat the Bully and suggested a reward of a candy bar if he finished the meal.

But mostly I wanted to de-dramatize the power that Timmy's worries had over his parents, especially Regina. In essence, I explained to them, the Bully was controlling not only Timmy but also *them*. They devoted a great deal of time to his fears, talking to Timmy about them, trying unsuccessfully to reassure him, and helping him avoid facing situations that made him uncomfortable. I asked them if they too were willing to resist the power of the Bully and help Timmy. Both said they were ready, but asked how.

"It's relatively simple. Try not to go out of your way to accommodate Timmy when the Bully is controlling him. You can even point out to Timmy that you aren't going to deal with him if the Bully is in charge." I wasn't telling them that they should deliberately stress their son with outrageous demands, like taking the BART train from Walnut Creek to San Francisco by himself. But for actions they knew he could perform—like retrieving a toy from his room in the evening, when it was dark—they could simply say, "If you want the toy you'll have to get it yourself. I think you can beat the Bully on this one."

Other parents have worried that this approach shuts them out from their child's mind, so I gave Regina an additional technique. I told her to offer Timmy five minutes of "worrying time," in which Timmy could show he was in charge of the Bully by intentionally bringing him into his mind for five minutes and sharing all his current, previous, and future worries with his mother. Most OCD patients complain that the worrying thoughts are intrusive: They come and go without the patient's control. We were asking Timmy to invite—no, to demand—that the Bully enter his head. In other words, he would control the Bully.

His mother's job was to listen and try to understand as completely as possible Timmy's concerns. However, she was specifically not to reason with him, reassure him, or deny his worries. After five minutes, the topic of conversation was to end. Timmy had to show her that he was the "boss" of the Bully and chase him away. If Timmy didn't stop talking about his worries after five minutes, he could continue thinking about them on his own but *she* would no longer listen. If he insisted on telling her about them she should send him to his room, where he was allowed to worry as much as he wanted.

Regina liked this approach very much. She wanted to listen to her son, but she also appreciated the notion of telling him "enough is enough." She frequently became frustrated with and tired of Timmy's constant complaints but until now had felt too anxious and guilty to tell him to stop. Only when her frustration reached gargantuan proportions would she then yell at him—at which point she felt even guiltier. She found this structure and control over the Bully appealing. Bill could do the same, but I suggested that Regina spend at least five minutes every evening inviting the Bully into their lives and then telling Timmy to kick the Bully out.

Regina and Timmy came in a week later. They were both very pleased and eager to tell me about their successes over the Bully. Timmy was eating his sandwiches regularly at school and was getting a candy bar as a reward every afternoon when he came home. The day before, though, he had a minor setback. He had eaten only half his sandwich. I told him to watch out: "The Bully is sneaky and can come back sometimes when you're having a bad day or someone's been mean to you." Timmy got my meaning exactly and agreed with a giggle.

Regina was even more pleased about the five minutes of worrying time. She had conscientiously gone home and explained the procedure to Timmy and had spent five minutes every evening since then talking with him about his worries. She was surprised when, over the last two or three nights, he had much less to talk about. More importantly, he was not complaining about his fears so much at other times. Once she had to send him to his room when he wouldn't stop telling her about some of his fears later on in the evening. I told Timmy that sounded tough, but I also told him that I was glad that the Bully could no longer control his mother so that she could help him more.

Bill, Regina, and Timmy returned a week later. Bill was very pleased over his son's progress. Timmy seemed lighter and so did Bill. Timmy was eating his entire lunch every day and had stopped the repetitious hand washings (even though we had not even addressed that particular behavior). Regina and he still did their five minutes every evening but lately had been talking about positive events of their day rather than his worries.

I told them I was pleased but reminded them to beware of sneak Bully attacks. Everyone has good days and bad days, and I saw Timmy's level of worry as a barometer of his emotional state. I knew he was doing better at the moment, but the improvements had been so astonishingly rapid that I was a bit skeptical. I told them to keep up the good work, and we scheduled a visit for the next month. They were to call me in the interim if there were any relapses.

A month later, they returned. Timmy continued to do well. "The Bully is bothering someone else now," he told me. Indeed, Timmy said he was not even thinking about germs any more, the clearest indicator that he had for now overcome his obsessive thoughts. Regina told me she attributed Timmy's success to my belief that he and his parents could do something about the OCD. Bill agreed. Regina added that she wasn't worried about the future; she felt that she and Timmy had developed tools and techniques for dealing with his problems. They had worked this time, and they could work again if necessary. In a small ceremony with his parents I awarded Timmy a certificate of achievement for "beating the Bully," something I do at times to honor a family's achievement. Kids like it and the parents like it even more.

The successful use of externalization requires the parents to be firm about how much time the "enemy" can hang around. By reviewing past successes, looking for examples of the child's competence in "battle," they learn that they may hold their child to a reasonable standard of behavior. Although it asks parents to be strong, the exercise is positive and fun. Most obvious candidates for this method are those suffering from unusual compulsions and rituals (like Timmy) and anxious kids who are deeply fearful, especially if they have the sensation of being bossed around by feelings they don't like.

Children with symptoms of ADHD or ODD can also be helped by externalization, but their cognitive, wanting-to-follow-the-rules sides can be overwhelmed by the impulsive or defiant aspects of their nature.

In these cases, I may rely on externalization as a way for parents to separate the bad behavior from the child. It also communicates to parents their need to control the problem that in turn is controlling their son or daughter. I worked once with a seven-year-old girl who decided to call her anger and misbehavior "Chicken Legs." The name became a code for her parents, who would use it to remind the girl when her behavior was becoming unacceptable. "Watch out for Chicken Legs," they'd say, or, "If you want to spend time with Chicken Legs, you'll need to take her up to your room. Chicken Legs can't come down here with us." If, despite their warnings, Chicken Legs stuck around, her parents employed a time-out, ending with the girl being very firmly escorted to her room.

A final word on Timmy. His family asked me if I could use the same technique to help their teenage daughter, who had been under separate psychiatric care for several years. Lately she had been caught shoplifting and subsequently tried to commit suicide by taking a bottle of Tylenol. Although I was ready to continue work with their family, I did not feel that this teenager would necessarily respond to a cognitive-behavioral approach that used externalization. Her problems clearly ran very deep and even posed an immediate threat to her and her family's health. She was already taking two medications, and I wondered whether her problems could be managed at home. This additional insight also helped me understand that Timmy's obsessive hand washing was probably linked to pressures inside the family—his sister's troubles, his father's sadness, and other psychological stresses. Externalization is not a panacea that could soothe away these problems. Additional work with the family was in order, and I was uncertain I could help. But at least Timmy was doing better. Using an externalization approach helped Timmy and his parents conquer his obsession, and it showed that he (and they) had the inner resources to handle additional stresses. Although a drug like Prozac might have assisted him over this bumpy patch as well, it would not have given him the sense of accomplishment and confidence that I hope will stand him well through future challenges.

6

How Can Teachers and Schools Help?

Enlisting the aid of schools and teachers is an essential step in a multifaceted approach to helping children. Kids who elicit complaints about disruptive classroom behavior are obvious candidates for parent–teacher cooperation, but even kids who have little trouble in the classroom (think of Timmy, the compulsive but affable hand washer) benefit when parents, teachers, and other experts join forces. And since behavioral and emotional problems often mask or accompany learning disabilities, unveiling and addressing learning issues may be a key component of your child's improvement.

School systems are equipped with several resources for children with educational or behavioral weaknesses. There are many popular school-based strategies; although some of these are of dubious benefit, others offer the kind of targeted assistance that makes a real difference.

Where to Begin: Evaluations, IEPs, 504 Plans, and In-class Accommodations for Learning Problems

Two federal laws—the Individuals with Disabilities Education Act (IDEA) and Section 504 of the Vocational Rehabilitation Act of 1973—mandate a process of evaluation and remediation for children with learning problems. Since at least 30 to 40 percent of children with behavior problems also have learning problems, and since many behavioral problems at school will disappear or decrease if educational difficulties are addressed, I believe a minimum educational assessment should occur *before* any psychological evaluation is performed. This is true for all children who are struggling but especially for those who did not experience troubles until their school career began. It is within your rights as a parent to request an assessment for learning difficulties at any time. Teachers, psychologists, and doctors can also request one, with the parents' approval. Because school assessments and evaluations are paid for with public funds and are required if a child is to receive special services, most parents choose to start with the school's tests.

When preliminary testing, called a student study team (SST) assessment, indicates a learning problem, the school must conduct a more thorough evaluation. Afterward, school personnel and parents meet to discuss the results and come up with a plan that meets the child's individual needs. If a child meets a certain degree of disability, usually performing at least two grade levels below his age or ability as measured on psychometric tests, the school must provide an individualized education plan (IEP). It may include in-school tutoring or special teachers and classes. Parents have approval over the IEP, which is reviewed every year, and the school is legally bound to honor its tenets. When a child does not qualify for an IEP, a school plan may nevertheless be covered under the provisions of Section 504; the interventions here are generally less intense and less costly. A 504 plan, like an IEP, binds the school in writing.

Both plans can include any of a wide array of techniques for learning problems, more than I can discuss here, but most of them present alternative methods of learning material. Many of these methods can be adopted inside the regular classroom, and Section 504 plans are usually limited to in-class accommodations. Sometimes teachers simplify their instructions and make certain the child understands them, as in the case of Reese Gardner, or teachers may add visual cues to verbal ones. Children may receive preferential seating near the front of the class or by the teacher's desk, or written notes provided in addition to lectures. Kids are often given more time to complete their tests and assignments, or they may be graded on effort in addition to performance. When these relatively unobtrusive but significant changes are made—especially if they occur in combination with effective parenting at home—both grades and behavior may take a turn for the better.

Most educators, parents, and pediatric specialists, including me, feel that the ideal educational environment for a child is that which is least restrictive but still provides an optimal amount of support. When in-class efforts are not successful, or when learning problems are serious or compounded by severe behavior issues, parents and teachers may draw on resources outside the regular classroom, ranging from pull-out classes to day-long special programs and even alternative schools. Balancing the degree of restriction against the amount of specialized attention a child will receive in these programs is a tricky business for most parents, and I present the options outside the regular classroom in more detail later in this chapter.

In theory, the IEP and 504 plans are solid, useful tools, and I have seen many kids helped by smart customized plans. But I would be remiss if I failed to mention that some parents encounter frustrating experiences. They may feel the wheels of evaluation grind exceedingly slow or wonder if the school's suggestions bear the shape of a cookie cutter. Most school personnel have genuinely good intentions, but the pressures on our education systems are enormous. Higher standards, decreasing tolerance for social passing, and even the proliferation of IEPs and 504 plans—although all laudable—can feel like so many boulders heaped atop a teacher's already heavy load. At the administrative level, cost and staffing issues may affect which services can realistically be offered. And principals and superintendents must negotiate a variety of conflicting social prerogatives. We may want special attention for our child but not want him stigmatized; we want better special education but not at the expense of the regular classroom; we want to accommodate kids with special needs within the general education classroom but not distract the other children from their learning.

Given this environment, the best of intentions may not be enough. And since everyone involved in the process is a human being, the exchange between parents and school can sometimes feel quite adversarial. At these times, it can be especially useful to consult an outside specialist, who can perform an evaluation and encourage the wheels to turn a little faster. At a school meeting, a specialist can help parents digest the sometimes technical information, cool down a charged atmosphere, or introduce new strategies to the school's existing repertoire. If you do not choose to hire a specialist, I encourage you to have your spouse or even a friend join you for these meetings. At the minimum, there will be two pairs of ears to listen to the sometimes overwhelming quantity of information provided by the three or four school personnel who are usually present. During the meeting, bear in mind that anything you agree to or sign can be changed at any time if you are uncomfortable or unhappy with it later.

Behavioral Accommodations Within the Regular Classroom

Learning interventions are often the best assistance a school can provide for a struggling child. But if behavioral problems are *not* accompanied by learning difficulties, it is still quite possible to work with teachers and schools. Sometimes only small adjustments are all that's needed in the classroom. Timmy, the child who obsessively washed his hands, was helped by a teacher who was cued into the externalization technique. She agreed to limit the amount of worrying Timmy could do aloud and offered him immediate distractions of work and fun. Ryan Cash, who suffered from impulsivity but did not have a learning problem, did much better when Mrs. Grey adopted the star sticker program, which employed rewards as well as punishments that were prompt instead of delayed. I have found that most elementary school teachers are willing to give this kind of approach—if not stickers, then another system of concrete, immediate rewards and punishments—a try.

Although violent or threatening behavior may require more serious actions, such as placement in a special class or a different school (I discuss both later), sometimes kids on the verge of expulsion can remain inside the standard classroom when parents, schools, and health professionals put their heads together, as you'll see below.

Evan, the Exploding Boy

I met Evan and his family in March, when Evan's school was threatening to kick him out of seventh grade. The alternative county schools that he might attend instead were not much of an alternative—either a partial day program or one that met only once a week—and both Evan and his parents wanted him to stay where he was. Yet Evan's behavior presented serious challenges. In the most recent episode, Evan's math teacher reprimanded him for making faces at a classmate. Although the initial offense was minor, Evan denied the charge. "You're picking on me," he cried. "I'm not the only one!" The teacher, feeling his authority publicly challenged, issued an ultimatum: Apologize or leave the class. Evan yelled again and threw his pencil at the floor. He left the classroom and remained absent for two more classes. When he returned, he told his teachers that he was on the athletic fields, "hanging out." This was the most dramatic occurrence in a pattern of yelling and running out of class.

His parents told me that Evan also stormed out of a meeting with his teachers and the vice principal to draw up a behavior contract. He felt that he was being set up "to get kicked out of school" and that everyone, especially his math teacher, was against him. (Evan had been included in the meeting from the very beginning, as the adults tried to hash out their differences. Usually I propose that the group work out a plan and a unified position without the child present, bringing him in only at the end.) Evan's parents were embarrassed by his behavior at the meeting, but they felt their boy had correctly picked up on an intent to "get rid" of him.

Evan spoke to me reluctantly. He blamed his teachers for his problems but agreed that he wanted to stay at the school. He was a stocky twelve-year-old, built like a fire plug, and it was easy to imagine that he'd look threatening when angry. Even his parents seemed cowed by him. They would patiently and endlessly attempt to reason with Evan and would often placate his demands to avoid a blowout at home, when he'd scream and hit his fists against the wall. His older brother was in high school and also had significant problems with acting-out behavior in middle school. He was diagnosed with ADHD and treated with Ritalin for two years. However, he had been accepted at a respected private school; according to the parents, he "had matured" and was doing well now without any medication.

After an evaluation lasting several sessions, I felt that Evan was prototypic of what is being popularly labeled the "explosive child"—a category comprising inflexible, superintense children who are unable to utilize the usual rewards and consequences for poor behavior because they go into a "vapor lock" of irrational anger. When other elements of his history were considered, Evan might also have qualified for bipolar disorder, an increasingly popular and highly controversial diagnosis in childhood. But on a practical level, I described Evan as hypersensitive. He would become anxious when teachers confronted him for trivial acting-out behaviors and felt trapped verbally, logically, and physically. His mind would freeze up in an attitude of "they're against me." Sensing potential humiliation in front of his peers, he would defend himself to the death—and make his situation worse with every minute.

Previous educational assessments had found him a capable student academically, although a minor developmental weakness made written work more difficult. For a kid with a more even temperament, this weakness wouldn't have been a big deal, but with Evan, a small frustration could build into a huge reaction, especially when he was asked to do reports or other long writing assignments. The school had already made some accommodations in this realm: Evan didn't have to write out math problems (just the answers), and his parents were permitted to type out some of his other work on their word processor. The changes had helped somewhat, and I did not think they needed to make any further accommodations along these lines. From my perspective, it was nice to know that both the school and parents had already demonstrated their willingness to make changes.

In our meetings, Evan and I externalized his problem as the "Unfairness Thing"—a code for his sense of injustice and heightened sensitivity to being singled out, both of which could take over his behavior. We worked on a message to the Unfairness Thing: "Whatever it is, it ain't worth it" to get that mad; some of his other behaviors led me to monitor him for depressive symptoms that can appear on the flip side of aggressive, acting-out behavior. His parents and I worked on holding firm with limits, and I found that his father had a real knack for offering choices that were elegant in their simple and limited nature: "You'll do this now or in the next fifteen minutes, or otherwise you'll be in your room for the rest of the night. Don't test me. Any questions?" By giving Evan a short window in which to take the requested action, his father allowed him some time to make the internal adjustments that were so difficult for him.

An intervention with school personnel was also critical, since expulsion was a constant risk and the alternative public schools were unacceptable to the family. Evan, his parents, and I agreed on a plan to propose to the school: When Evan began losing control in the classroom, his teacher would give him a warning. Evan could respond in one of two ways. He could either calm down and stay in the room ("It ain't worth it" to get that mad, he might tell the Unfairness Thing) or, if he preferred, he could leave the class briefly, for five minutes or less, to collect himself. Then he was to return with no mention made by either the teacher or Evan about the incident. If Evan chose to stay in the room but did not calm down, his teacher would order him to leave for five minutes. Should he refuse, the teacher was to call the office and someone preassigned to this duty would escort him to the office. If he resisted physically or ran off, his parents would be called and one of them would have to take him home for the day. School personnel would not try to soothe Evan or reason with him, since those efforts appeared to have contributed to escalations in the past. If the parents had to be called more than twice in a short period of time, the plan would be considered unsuccessful and an alternative school placement would be considered.

Evan liked the plan because it gave him a face-saving way to collect himself. It also kept him from feeling trapped, which he said was a key element of his previous behavior. Although calling a school meeting was difficult after the previous disaster, the school found the plan acceptable and each of his teachers signed on. (Such a plan would be harder, but not impossible, to enact for older kids, since many teachers feel that this kind of special adaptation should not be necessary in high school.)

The plan was a success—Evan never even had to leave the classroom! He did get reminders from the teachers, but their warnings were short and he didn't challenge them. In addition to feeling less trapped, Evan felt better that he had worked cooperatively to develop the agreement. He also recognized on a gut level that the school had reached its limit; continued pushing from him would surely result in expulsion. Evan, his parents, and I saw each other on a regular basis until the end of the school year. Within a few months, even his grades improved. During the summer, his family and I decided we could take a break and then see what happened at the start of the next school year.

This group of interventions allowed Evan to stay in school and improved life for both him and his family. However, they did not completely resolve his problems. After Christmas vacation the following year, Evan started making his parents miserable at home with renewed challenges and explosions. Three weeks later, he was suspended for losing his temper in the classroom.

In the office, Evan was visibly down. In contrast to the defiant boy I had seen the previous year, Evan literally hung his head and shoulders. His speech was slower, sadder. He was even willing to admit he was making mistakes. Eventually, I offered him Zoloft, a Prozac-like drug that could possibly make him more resilient to small insults and therefore less likely to respond with an explosive reaction. I was also concerned about statements he was making: "I hate myself," he said to his parents during a regretful postmeltdown recovery period. Even more distressing was, "Your lives would be so much better if I just wasn't around." I thought medication might improve his mood, and, after some initial hesitation, he agreed to try the Zoloft. Together with his mother, we defined goals for him of fewer displays of anger, crying, and whining.

I turned again to the school. This time, the school psychologist was far less amenable. He had received several formal letters of complaint from teachers who wanted Evan out of their classes. They felt physically threatened. A third round of school meetings was scheduled, and despite my lowered expectations, they went unexpectedly well. His eighth-grade teachers, as it turned out, had not yet been clued into last year's successful plan. Once they heard about it, they were willing to employ it once more. That's something both parents and therapists should remember: Each year, there may be a new round of teachers to "educate." Among medication, our meetings, and school, things improved again for Evan.

Eventually, Evan decided to leave the public school system after middle school for the private high school his brother attended. It was a natural transition for a child in his community and not driven solely by his difficulties; many of Evan's friends also left the public system at this age. I contributed a letter to his application package to explain some of Evan's erratic behavior and offered that I thought this particular school environment would be ideal for Evan in its structure, sense of pride, and support. As of this writing, Evan has been at his new high school for three months. He is enjoying the school and is not taking the Zoloft; he says that he doesn't feel he needs it and believes it gives him trouble sleeping. His parents, who would prefer that Evan remain on Zoloft, nevertheless agree that he is doing well for now.

Options Outside the Regular Classroom

Children with serious, persistent learning and behavioral problems may not see significant improvement simply with alterations to the regular classroom environment. At this point, parents must weigh their alternatives. Most demand sacrifices in terms of social stigma, financial cost, travel logistics, or other matters, all of which must be taken into account. To find a balance between giving your child appropriate educational support while imposing no more restriction than necessary, you'll need to keep close tabs on your child's progress and be willing to work with the teacher as well as an outside consultant. Wise and experienced parents tell me that when kids have been struggling for a long time, the perfect fit between child and learning environment can be maddeningly elusive. You may need to aim for compromises that you, your child, and your family can best live with.

If support and accommodations inside the regular classroom fail, most schools will suggest a "pull-out" for "resource" (the current term for special education). Under ideal circumstances, a child who has, say, difficulty with reading will be "pulled out" of the regular class when reading is being taught. But lining up children's schedules with the special ed teacher's schedule is not often possible. No matter when the instruction occurs, a child in resource will work with a specially trained teacher, usually in a very small group of two or three other kids but sometimes one-on-one. Their work will focus on the child's weakness; for example, the teacher may slow down the phonics approach to reading so that the child can learn to process the elements of language. At the elementary school level, there is little stigma attached to resource. For middle and high school students, resource may be just one of many classes in their schedule. Most of the other kids don't care as much as the child's parents do.

If a child is spending up to 50 percent of the day in pull-out programs and still does not see success, the next option is a special day class, or SDC. The advantages of SDCs include small classes—which should not include more than twelve students but often do—as well as a full-time special education teacher plus an aide. Some children, usually the ones with serious educational problems rather than behavioral ones, do quite well in this protected environment. The intense classroom management may also allow the most difficult of children, who deserve education and are entitled to it, to remain in the regular school.

It is not surprising that such a structured, specialized option also has drawbacks. There's no evidence that SDCs produce better long-term outcomes than other programs do in terms of completing high school or avoiding delinquency and substance abuse.

The child's classmates may include students with even greater troubles, so parents who are considering SDCs should visit the class and see it in action. Social stigma is another legitimate concern.

A deciding factor for many parents is that the gains made by a child within an SDC often do not translate if the child is switched back into a regular classroom. Without the extra support of the specialized environment, the child's problems may reemerge. The chances of maintaining the success once the child is inside the normal class are better if the teacher receives training and assistance in behavioral and educational techniques tailored for the child. You may wish to discover in advance whether such assistance is offered. I know several families who have rejected SDCs because they are afraid that once in, the child will remain there for the rest of his educational life. They are also alarmed by the much higher dropout rate for kids in SDCs than those in the general student population. To be fair, the problem is circular: The children who wind up in SDCs are also the ones with problems that may predispose them toward leaving school.

In the end, the decision to place a child in an SDC is never easy; parents need to weigh continued failure in the regular classroom and pull-out programs against the chance of success in the special day class. They may also face a tough choice between a restrictive educational environment and medication.

The lack of success in returning SDC students to the regular classroom has prompted some schools to address the needs of special education children within the regular classroom. This movement, known as "full inclusion," includes the use of parent volunteers, teacher aides, and assistance from special education teachers who try to adapt the classroom environment for the child in need. When all these elements are in place and working, full inclusion can be a boon for both the struggling child *and* the other children in the class. But even when this option is available, it's not necessarily the best solution for every kid; some children, families, and administrators continue to feel that the restrictive specialized education option provides a necessary level of intensity and classroom management.

SEEKING THE SHADOW: AN ELUSIVE IN-CLASS OPTION

For distractible, impulsive kids whose learning problems make it even harder for them to focus, some schools have adopted the use of an aide, or "shadow," who assists the child inside the regular classroom. When the child's attention or control wanders away, the aide responds immediately to help the child stay focused. In most cases, the aide is responsible for just one child, although in some classes there may be several kids on the aide's watch. I like shadows as an alternative to pulling children out of the standard classroom. They work especially well for elementary school children. The rigorous, intensive help appears to teach them coping skills, and in the lower grades there is little social stigma attached. Even for children in secondary school, an aide may result in less disruption and social discomfort than placement in a special class.

Although aides are among the most effective means of keeping a difficult child in the mainstream classroom, administrators are often reluctant to provide them. They're simply too expensive for most school budgets; it's much cheaper to send a child for special instruction or even to a special school rather than hire a full-time aide. Nevertheless, if a school raises the possibility of an SDC for your child, go ahead and inquire if the administration is willing to bring in a shadow instead. Your chances may be slim, but who knows? And sometimes parents are able to hire shadows at their own expense.

If SDCs or full inclusion do not work, some districts have schools for children who are developmentally delayed or severely emotionally disturbed. These schools offer more specialized environments, with trained teachers as well as full-time psychologists, social workers, or even psychiatrists on the premises. But the schools are usually at some distance from the child's home, and the child will be with other severely troubled or disabled kids.

Private Schools

Private schools are a popular option these days for those who can afford it, even in middle-class suburbs that boast supposedly "good" public schools. If asked, I tell parents that I prefer the parochial Catholic schools (which surprises people, since I am Jewish). They offer continued exposure to a strong moral system, one that provides an alternative to the rampant consumerist mentality in most public schools. Students in parochial schools seem to feel more protected and buoyed; in a positive twist on peer pressure, they may assimilate the school's values and assert them in the presence of one another. Secular private schools, with their smaller class sizes and more individual attention, can be another good choice. Some offer specialized educational options similar to those in public schools, but parents should be aware that private schools in general tend to draw high-achieving students rather than those with learning problems. The academic pressure may be more intense.

In some communities, there are private schools for learning disabled or behaviorally disturbed kids. There's also something of a growth industry in private and extremely pricey boarding schools for acting-out adolescents, but the research on the outcomes kids experience in these settings is equivocal. I prefer not to send adolescents away, but there are times when the normal environment of home and school cannot provide the immediacy and monitoring necessary to keep a teen safe—unless his compliance can be gained chemically, often at the expense of sedation or other side effects (and a really angry, disturbed kid usually refuses medication in any case).

Although Evan, the boy described earlier in this chapter, was able to navigate public middle school with a fair degree of success, his parents decided that a secular private high school offered more structure and individual support, with a lower student–teacher ratio. Their decision was made easier by their older son's success in this environment and by the family's ability to pay the tuition. Some parents I know have considered private schools and rejected them, feeling that the financial burden would cause even more stress on the family or force a currently at-home parent to work. (In very rare cases, the public school district will agree to pay for a child's private school tuition; obviously, the school district must feel that the child has exhausted all the available public facilities and also weigh the cost of one child's tuition—which may equal a teacher's salary—against the needs of all the other kids). Other parents have decided that their child would suffer too much from the loss of current school friends or would not have anyone to play with at home. All of these concerns are valid, and I have backed the families in their decisions. Other potential drawbacks, such as increased travel time, must be taken into account.

The Plum Class: Special Program, Private School

Paul and Alice Robertson were referred to me by a psychologist who had diagnosed Christina, their third grader, with ADHD-inattentive type. The psychologist thought I should further investigate the possibility of using Ritalin. When I spoke with the parents, I discovered that they were split on the issue: Alice was ready to try medication, but Paul wanted a second opinion. Their story demonstrates some of the ground that parents must negotiate when thinking about both special classes and private schools.

We talked about Christina's problems. The teacher at her private school had complained that the girl failed to complete her in-class assignments, was unfocused in the classroom, and did not turn in her homework. She felt that Christina belonged in something called the Plum Class, a day-long special education program. Although her placement in this new class was the impetus for the psychological evaluation, Christina's problems were actually greater at home. She was lovable, the parents said, enthusiastic and lively, but she required constant supervision. She hated transitions and would fuss and cry when it was time to go to school or leave the park for home. Neither she nor her younger sisters (aged seven and five) could sit through a dinner meal with their parents. Her parents admitted that they weren't especially consistent with their discipline. Their grueling work hours made it difficult: Both parents put in more than fifty hours a week. They looked worn down, especially Christina's mother, whose sighs and tears indicated major burnout to me.

As if to prove the parents' statements, the family meeting was marked by general chaos, with the kids wandering in and out of conversation and walking about the room as we all tried to talk. "Will you girls come back here?" Alice repeatedly called from the couch, but the children ignored her. Paul arrived at the meeting twenty minutes late, apologizing and a little out of breath as he took off his jacket. He tended to cede control to his wife in matters of discipline, although he sighed and shifted his posture to convey irritation with his children's level of activity. I did not notice much difference between Christina's behavior and that of her two younger sisters. I could sympathize with this family's exhaustion and desire for help.

Christina's family left the room, and I met with the girl alone. She was a sweet-looking child; her dark hair, cut into a short pixie style, emphasized her impish qualities. At first she chatted idly in a baby voice and swung her feet from the chair, casting her glance about the room. But about five minutes into our conversation, she seemed to mature by about two or three years. She sat taller, with less fidgeting, and she spoke to me in clear and competent tones. After my education screening, I found that I basically agreed with the psychologist's educational assessment. Christina's intelligence was normal, but she had a marked difficulty with auditory processing. She was also totally dependent on using her fingers for adding and subtracting. Despite the teacher's reports of her classroom behavior, Christina proceeded methodically about her work on the tests; I saw none of the impulsive guessing that, among other things, had led the psychologist to consider her a candidate for ADHD.

I believed Christina could be successful without medication. It seemed clear that the entire family was likely to see real benefit from more limits at home. What clinched things was my conversation with the head teacher of the Plum Class. There were only twelve kids in the class, with three teachers. The students' problems were predominantly with learning rather than with seriously disturbed behavior, a significant advantage over the special day classes in many public (and some private) schools. The teacher reported that Christina was well-liked by her new classmates; when I asked if there were any conflicts with her and the adults, the teacher seemed a bit surprised. There had been none—quite a contrast with the behavior problems her parents experienced at home. Christina was given work more appropriate to her skill level and was monitored closely; under these circumstances, work completion and focus were no longer problems. The Plum Class teachers also used tangible rewards (marbles that the kids could collect for prizes either as individuals or in table groups).

I thought this learning situation was ideal for Christina and could not offer ways to improve on what they were doing. I only wished more kids could be in Christina's situation. I realized that the program cost more money, and there was some stigma, especially for the parents, attached to this program.

Paul and Alice agreed with me that Christina was doing better in the new class, but they were concerned that she would learn less. However, they recognized that in the high-powered environment of the regular private school classroom, Christina might well have needed a stimulant to keep up—an option that her parents decided compromised their best hopes for Christina. We briefly discussed sending Christina to public school, where the broader range of abilities among the kids might allow her to find a place within a regular classroom, but in the end the Robertsons felt that the private school offered a better education and social environment. I continued to work with the parents, framing the need for more immediate and effective discipline in terms of their children's cravings for security.

Questionable Interventions

Much of the time, successful school interventions come down to the individuals—the child, parents, teacher, and others—who are directly involved. But I have found some routine interventions to be less useful, no matter how dedicated the team. Regular meetings between the child and the school psychologist or counselor are one example. There is little evidence that talk or play therapy does much more than offer emotional support, which can be accomplished through the occasional "checking-in" appointment. Weekly or biweekly appointments, in my experience, do not provide much additional help. An exception occurs when a child has been recently exposed to trauma, such as abuse, divorce, or persistent bullying and victimization; in these cases, more frequent visits may be advisable.

Another popular strategy is the "rainbow group," a euphemism for difficult kids who meet on a regular basis with the counselor. The children are encouraged to share their problems and solutions with one another. They might also play a game. These groups are a little better than individual meetings, since the kids are at least practicing some social skills under the guidance of a trained adult. In general, I think it would be a much wiser use of public money and limited personnel if the school counselor or psychologist met with the child initially and then for the occasional follow-up visit. The counselor would be free to spend more time assisting the child's teacher and developing an integrated plan with the parents' involvement. This professional could suggest behavioral management techniques, accommodations for learning problems, and other means of effective support for the child *in the classroom*. Too often, no one suggests such techniques to the teacher until an outside expert makes some noise.

What Can Parents Do?

Parents often want to know what they can do to improve their child's behavior and performance at school. In some ways, the answer is: frustratingly little. Talking to the child about the problem tends to be ineffective, as is offering rewards or punishments for school behavior, since the parental consequences are usually too time-delayed for the kids. (An exception is a system like the star sticker program, described earlier in this book, in which a teacher issues stars for good behavior; the parent may present a reward at home when a predetermined number of stars is collected during the week. But in this case, the sticker itself is the immediate reward for the child and is as significant as the toy or special privilege given later.)

What parents can do is inform themselves of the educational options available for their child. You can lobby your consultant to work with the school; if that doesn't happen, you may wish to find another or—keeping in mind that we all live in the real world and that not all specialists will be willing to help out at school—try to brainstorm with the teacher and school personnel on your own, ideally in the company of the child's other parent. But the best, most important effort you can make is to support both the child and the school by reinforcing appropriate classroom behavior and good study habits at home. Keeping your expectations high, using fewer words and choices, and responding with immediacy as well as action will prepare your child for life in the social environment of school.

7

When Is Enough Enough?

I rarely believe that a child *must* take a psychiatric drug. There are almost always other choices, which change a child's environment instead of her biochemistry. But for kids with severe problems, many of those environmental choices, like restrictive classrooms or even group homes and psychiatric hospitals, come with their own set of problems that make medication appear more desirable. Even when a child's difficulties are less serious, the use of a psychiatric medication in a treatment plan can still make sense. (However, if parents strongly oppose using a medication even when I believe it may be helpful, I will aid and support sensible alternatives.)

The decision to employ medication is, as always, one of balancing the degree of the child's problems against the drug's proven or unproven efficacy and side effects. I discuss specific medication classes and brands elsewhere in this book, but here I note that many of the psychoactive drugs currently used in children have no proven track record of effectiveness or safety in the pediatric population. Consequently, the child's problems must be severe enough, and resistant enough to other interventions, to justify the unknown risks involved.

But I also keep in mind that untreated problems can have their own negative outcomes, ranging from a worrisome erosion of the child's self-confidence to physical harm. In the next few paragraphs I provide a series of examples in which the particular circumstances of a child, family, and wider environment led me to say "enough is enough," in other words, to offer medication. These scenarios may give you a sense of when, for me, a child's circumstances tip the scales toward certain drugs. And when I prescribe medication, I continue to encourage nondrug strategies. Even if a child is taking a pill that seems to help, parents must work to create a home environment that offers love, stability, and limits, and both learning problems and discipline issues must be addressed in the classroom.

During the family visit portion of his evaluation, seven-year-old Tony was impulsive and fidgety. His parents were rather passive and unclear about discipline, and I wondered what would happen if they set limits with greater consistency. However, the family appeared to be a strong, loving unit, with no apparent major problems (like an impending divorce or serious financial pressure) other than their difficult child. I talked to Tony's teacher, who seemed reasonable in her demands. Although she had not employed what I call a truly rigorous behavioral approach with Tony, she tried offering him stickers as a reward for good behavior and kept him seated near her so that she could help him stay on track. Despite her efforts, Tony continued to lose focus and drift away from class activities.

Many kids with behavior like Tony's sit nicely when they're alone with me in the office. When a child can control himself under one circumstance but not another, I muse: Could we take elements of the settings in which the child demonstrates success and replicate those elements in her other environments? Perhaps the highly structured, one-on-one experience with the doctor could be adapted elsewhere. Or if the child follows the rules in class but not at home, the parents might take a cue from the school's approach to discipline. (When asked why she had "grump attacks" only at home and never at school, a nine-year-old girl replied, "Why, Dr. Diller . . . there's no principal at home.")

Until twenty or even ten years ago, this approach prevailed in most medical and therapy offices. Replicating the circumstances of success is not meant to cast blame on parents or teachers; some children require a level of consistency, immediacy, and teaching that places extraordinary demands on the adults in their lives. But this approach offers a way of thinking about the problem that does not lead to medication as a first and only intervention. Nowadays, however, many professionals take a nearly opposite approach. It is widely believed that a child who can play, work, and hold a conversation perfectly well in the office—both with her family present and alone with the doctor—and can conduct herself at home can still be a candidate for medication if she has behavioral problems at school. Medication becomes a tool that is offered much more quickly.

But Tony, as it turned out, did not present himself with more composure when he was alone with me. When I tried to talk with him, he'd be falling off his chair, walking around the room, and trying to get into the toys. In the educational assessment portion of our meeting, he'd rock his chair back and forth and play with his pencil. (I took it away when he didn't need it.) He was so distracted by the sound of air conditioning that he hesitated in his reading and lost track of his place in the paragraph.

When a child's impulsivity or distractibility is so persistent and pervasive that it appears in nearly every setting—with parents, at school, alone with the doctor—I am much more likely to think of medication early in the process. Stimulants, the drugs used for ADHD-like symptoms, are unlike other psychoactive medications used for children in that they have a history of effectiveness and at least short-term safety. So I was ready to prescribe a drug to help Tony focus. I told his parents that the medication was not a substitute for more behavioral management at home and at school; in the long term, their efforts would be more important than the drug. But using medication from the get-go might make those efforts easier to set into motion.

Eight-year-old Vicki was by nature moderately distractible and impulsive; on top of her inborn temperament, she had some minor learning problems that made it even more difficult for her to focus on school assignments. After three months of earnest effort by her parents, Vicki's behavior at home settled down; she would usually pick up her toys when asked once or twice and became much less likely to pick fights with her sister. But Vicki's third-grade teacher, Miss Ray, reported that despite special tutoring for her learning difficulties, Vicki continued to talk back loudly and chat with her friends when she was supposed to be working. Miss Ray tried a system of immediate reinforcements for Vicki but abandoned it after a few weeks. She was simply too busy, she said, to change her teaching style and implement special rewards and punishments for just one child. Given her class size of thirty-one children, I could appreciate her dilemma. Vicki's parents looked into a private school nearby and liked what they saw, but they could not afford the tuition.

Vicki, although proud of her improvement at home, was increasingly frustrated with her continued difficulties at school: "I'm bad," she told me. I told her parents that I was prepared to offer Vicki a stimulant medication like Ritalin or Adderall for use during school hours. It would not remediate her learning problem, but it would help her maintain focus instead of drifting away when the work grew challenging. She would also act less impulsively and might use the teacher's rule system with success. Again, I am less reluctant to offer a stimulant medication for kids than any other drug, thanks to what we know about its effects. The result here was happy, if slightly compromised by the situation at school: With the combination of the stimulant, her parents' continued dedication, and the tutoring, Vicki had far fewer behavior problems in class. Her parents noticed further improvement at home when Vicki was taking the drug, even though the medication had worn off by the afternoon and their daughter was operating "on her own chemicals."

"Cut that crap out!" snapped Laura Cunningham. Jason, her four-year-old son, had been pounding toys into the floor since our meeting began half an hour ago. He destroyed things at home, and his preschool was threatening to kick him out. In a previous meeting, Laura had broken down in silent tears several times and was barely able to tell me about her son's problems. Today she reacted to her child's behavior in the office with a kind of tension that was very quiet and still. She reminded me of a string pulled tightly at both ends. "I feel like a failure," she said twice in a choked voice. Now, having erupted in harsh words toward Jason, she buried her face in her hands, her shoulders quaking.

"How do you think you could help your wife right now?" I asked her husband, who had not offered many comments so far. In response, he looked up toward the ceiling and opened his palms.

Here was a case of serious oxygen depletion, definitely for Laura and perhaps also for her husband. I felt that the family needed some immediate relief before they could work on providing Jason with the kind of environment that would help him. We focused on ways Laura could get air flowing into her lungs again, perhaps in the form of a kid-free vacation, regular exercise, or more help from her husband. Ultimately, I proposed medication—not for the child, but for Laura. I was worried about her continued stress level and signs of outright depression. After some time with the drug, along with concomitant changes in both parents' approach to discipline, Laura reported that Jason's problems, although still serious, no longer seemed overwhelming. She also felt capable of responding to his provocations more evenhandedly. As she began to carve out a middle ground between dead quiet and yelling, Jason's behavior improved.

I had been seeing fourteen-year-old Peter and his family for a while because of Peter's episodes of intense rage. After some initial success, Peter had an angry encounter with a teacher at school; afterward, he told his parents that he wished he were dead. When I questioned him specifically, Peter described a fantasy of lying out on the street and waiting for a car to run him over. He had never done it, he said, nor did he think that he would in the future. But I felt that the specificity of his fantasy, combined with other signs, signaled a disturbingly high level of distress. I offered him Zoloft to help his mood and resiliency. No study tells me for sure that a drug like Zoloft, which belongs to a class called selective serotonin reuptake inhibitors (SSRIs), helps teenagers, and we do not yet know what the long-term side effects of teen use might be. However, I do know the short-term effects of a suicide attempt or gesture.

I am more likely to consider medication in cases of suicidal fantasy and risk when a child is thirteen or older. Younger children rarely act out on these thoughts; this lower risk of harm from suicidal thinking makes me hesitant to take a chance with a medication's unknown side effects and effectiveness, especially since there are productive non-drug interventions for children who are unhappy. And younger kids simply don't respond to these drugs as well as adults or even teens do. However, if your child is talking about suicide, you should get a professional evaluation immediately, no matter what her age.

Peter's life improved, but elements of his environment changed as well. Consequently, it's hard for me to say whether the drug was a significant cause. He attended an Outward Bound camp for a month and reported having a very good experience there. I also learned that his mother had been worried all along that her son might kill himself, something she had not shared with me previously. She had been on eggshells around him, afraid to upset him with demands or with punishments for poor behavior. Once he was on the drug and we were talking openly about her fears, she felt much less like a hostage to what she perceived as her son's fragility and more comfortable setting clear limits for him. His mother felt certain that Peter was "more mellow" on the medication—little things bothered him less and he was more likely to recover quickly when he was upset. Peter himself was less sure how much help the drug had provided; his feelings about it varied from equivocal to positive.

David Mendelssohn, twelve years old, suffered from Tourette's syndrome. He had developed involuntary tics that took the form of eye blinking and facial grimacing—his mouth would open wide, as if he were yawning constantly, and he would occasionally make a series of grunting noises. An exquisitely self-conscious boy to begin with (too self-conscious to even talk about his self-consciousness), he was worried that his friends would think he was weird. He gathered up the courage to tell his mother about his worries, and she relayed them to me. David wasn't sure about medication at first, but eventually in the privacy of his home (his self-consciousness at work again) he told his mother that he would like to give it a try. I offered him clonidine, a drug that I discuss in detail elsewhere in this book. Clonidine, known primarily for its effects on hypertension, is also useful in childhood behavior problems and has been helpful for some kids with Tourette's syndrome.

David initially experienced a reduction of tics with the Clonidine. But they returned with greater frequency a year or so later, and I wound up offering David Haldol, a drug that sometimes causes unwanted movements (tardive dyskinesias) but, ironically, does not produce this effect when given in low doses for Tourette's. He and his mother reported that he was feeling better about himself with the Haldol; they also said that he experienced few to none of the sedating effects that this drug can often bring on. The last I heard from David, he was in his late teens. The tics had pretty much gone away and he had discontinued medication. I don't believe the Haldol helped make the tics disappear, but I do think that the medication supported him through a particularly rough patch of his growing up.

Taylor's foster parents told me that they could not control his aggressive behavior toward the other children under their care. He constantly broke their rules. It was a daily battle to get him off to school in the morning. Evenings were marred by his fights with the other kids, not to mention his regular outbursts and tantrums. He had bitten two of the other children already and broken the skin. Unless I prescribed drugs to calm Taylor, the parents said, they were going to send him on to another family. It would be the third foster home for this six-year-old in less than a year.

Taylor's situation was distressing. His intractability and his biting threatened the operation of what was, essentially, a group home for kids. His foster parents were to be commended for their efforts, but they were not especially warm people. They relied mostly on videos and television to keep the children occupied, and they were surprisingly naive in their expectations of self-management from the children in their home. The parents were so burdened by their tasks that they rarely had the time to separate Taylor from the other children and keep him at a distance until he calmed down. They had tried holding Taylor in place, as the social worker had suggested, but it hadn't worked for them.

The foster parents agreed to give nondrug approaches a try, and we worked on the quality of attention and affection in their home. But we made little progress. Despite the barely adequate conditions in his current foster home, I worried that Taylor would also be harmed by being bounced to yet another family. Given his violent outbursts, which could easily place him in the class of kids who meet the criteria for bipolar disorder, I decided to try an SSRI. When that didn't help much, I offered him a low dose of Risperdal, one of the newer antipsychotic medications. I used this big-gun medication with great reluctance and only because Taylor's environment was so lousy and so resistant to change that it seemed justified to me. Taylor ultimately remained with the family as I continued to monitor him for side effects. His weight increased over time (which often happens on Risperdal), but how else he was affected I don't know. I lost contact with the family after several months because of an insurance change. I am still unsure what kind of long-term effects the drug may have on Taylor's brain and body.

These cases may or may not reflect your situation: I offer them as a range of possibilities in which medication might be used. In the end, a doctor's decision to offer medication should be tailored to the needs of each and every child who comes to the office. The following chapter may help you learn more about medications and the times when they are indicated.

8

How Will the Medication
Affect Your Child?

Sometimes a child's personality is so extreme, or the environment in which the child lives or goes to school is so unyielding, that serious problems continue despite behavioral and learning interventions. If parents in these unenviable situations have made their best efforts at changing their child's world, they should not feel guilty about considering medication. But they need to enter this often uncharted territory with their eyes open.

Weighing the benefits of a psychoactive drug against the risks to the child is nerve-wracking for most parents. The input of a trusted doctor—perhaps two of them—can aid you at this time, but you also need information about the specific medication that is being considered. How much can it help? In what ways could it hurt? Has the drug been studied for its effects on children? What level of impairment or suffering justifies the risks that the child might incur?

Not all of these questions have straightforward, just-the-facts-ma'am answers. They are a matter of lively and sometimes ferocious debate among academicians, doctors, parents, teachers, politicians, and just about anyone else with a strong interest in children's health. In this chapter I try to give you a start, with information about the classes of psychoactive drugs most often prescribed to children. I have included my opinions about which drugs appear to be safe and effective and which are being used without appropriate testing on kids. For the sake of convenience, the two most popular drug classes—stimulants and the selective serotonin reuptake inhibitors (the class that includes Prozac and Zoloft)—are presented first and in the most detail. Less frequently used drug options, like antipsychotics or tricyclics, are described afterward. More information about specific brand names and preparations is available in the guide at the end of the book.

The Path to Pediatric Prescriptions:
What Parents Need to Know

Most psychiatric drugs have *not* been systematically studied for safety and effectiveness in children. As this book goes to press, the only drugs approved by the Food and Drug Administration for the treatment of psychiatric conditions in children are stimulants like Ritalin and two of the Prozac-like drugs. But most of the medications used to treat children's emotional problems first became available after they met FDA standards for psychiatric use in *adults*. A few were initially approved for adults with nonpsychiatric conditions like seizures and high blood pressure.

Once the FDA approves a drug for the treatment of a specific medical condition, a doctor may prescribe it "off label" for any purpose. Off-label use of medicines in pediatrics is common and not necessarily disturbing in and of itself, but it is never employed so frequently as for psychiatric drugs. Local hospital and medical boards usually do little to interfere with a doctor's treatment preferences, so the decision to prescribe a psychiatric medication for a child comes down to an individual physician's own judgment and ethics. Under these circumstances, parents are well-advised to learn as much as possible about the proposed medication.

How does a medication that has not been tested on kids achieve widespread acceptance and use? The typical path begins with a report of a single child's response to a drug, usually as a letter printed in one of the professional journals. A report may generate other letters until a series of case studies is reported. In the absence of better studies, such reports can have a certain amount of utility. But the usual rigorous scrutiny and peer review that precede publication of a full-blown article are omitted. In most case studies, all parties—doctor, parent, and child—know which drug is being used, a scientific weakness that can muddy our understanding of the drug's effects, both positive and unwanted.

Much more preferable is the Super Bowl of drug testing, the double-blind randomized control study (DBRCS). In a DBRCS neither the family nor the doctor knows whether the child is getting the medication or a placebo (an identical capsule filled with an inert ingredient). Only the pharmacist who prepares the medication knows which capsule contains the drug to be tested. Patients are carefully screened for the psychiatric condition to be treated and then are randomly selected to receive either the real drug or the placebo. Parents and doctors monitor the children for improvements and side effects; many children who take placebos show benefits or complain of unwanted effects like headache and stomachache. After a predetermined period it is revealed who took the drug and who did not. Only then does one learn the "real" versus "believed" effects of the drug. (In the only DBRCS of Prozac on children, 60 percent of the improvement in depressive symptoms was attributed to the placebo effect.)

These rigorous studies are expensive and, until recently, pediatric psychopharmacology researchers have been limited by low funds. The few DBRCSs that had been run usually included only enough children, often fewer than one hundred, to generate the likelihood of a statistically significant difference between drug and placebo required for scientific journal publication, but not enough for FDA approval. (FDA approval does not necessarily mean that a drug is more effective than other measures, simply that it is more powerful than a placebo.) Many studies have been conducted for no more than a few weeks, hardly long enough to determine long-term benefits or risks.

Are Pediatric Studies Really Necessary?

Even when a psychiatric drug has been approved for adults, study of its effects on kids is crucial. Kids have brains and bodies that are still under construction. Side effects that are manageable in adults might have far more serious long-term consequences for little ones. Nor are the benefits of a drug necessarily the same in both populations. For example, tricyclic drugs like imipramine, desipramine, and nortriptyline (the first-line pharmaceuticals for adult depression until Prozac came along) were initially used for similar problems in children. Then studies in the 1960s and 1970s demonstrated their lack of effectiveness for depressive symptoms in kids. Many theories are offered to account for this difference: somehow the developing brain is different from the mature brain; the young brain metabolizes the drug differently; the diagnosis of depression and other disorders is inaccurate in children; the environment has a much greater influence on children by virtue of their utter dependency on caregivers compared to adults. No clear proof of one theory over another exists. But the tricyclic experience demonstrates the need for separate studies in children.

Yet with only scores of children having been formally assessed for their responses to psychiatric medications at this time, drugs like Prozac, Risperdal, clonidine, and Wellbutrin have been prescribed for hundreds of thousands of kids. Perhaps we will soon see better testing. Advocates within the child mental health community are calling loudly for increased funding of pediatric psychopharmacology research. And the pharmaceutical industry, which now sees a children's market large enough to justify the expense—and which stands to benefit from a new law that extends drug patents by six months if the company tests the medicine for pediatric use—is funding many large studies. Nonetheless, it is not necessarily wise to rely on studies supported by an industry that stands to profit by certain outcomes. In other drug trials funded by the industry, there has been evidence of "spin" and even suppression of negative findings.

Even when a drug is approved for use in children, or when a new drug comes on the market touting safety and fewer side effects, families and doctors should remember the "five-year rule" of psychiatric medications, which an experienced colleague once shared with me: "Prescribe a new medication in the first five years, before the full extent of side effects are known," he said. "In the second five years, you'll become more cautious because the drug's effectiveness and safety will start to look similar to the older drugs available for the condition. But by the third five years, you won't be prescribing the drug at all because its patent will have expired and a new drug promoting better effectiveness and fewer side effects will be offered." True drug advances are rare, although they do happen. My colleague's cynical advice is a reminder about continuing hopes, potential manipulation, and exploitation.

THE POWER OF THE PHARMACEUTICAL INDUSTRY

I suggest that parents cultivate an awareness of the pharmaceutical industry's power to influence the way we view and respond to our children's problems. In 2001, drug companies began advertising directly to parents via magazines and television. Under the guise of "education," these ads promote a particular—and profitable—perspective of children's behavior: Problems are the result of a brain-based condition and require a drug "fix." At least one ad reduces difficulty completing homework—in actuality a complex developmental and social undertaking—to a disorder to be solved by a pill.

Advertising works on doctors too. After three years of a relentless campaign directed at physicians by the makers of Adderall, doctors are now prescribing this stimulant more frequently than any other, including Ritalin. Professional conventions are virtually run on "drug money." I am regularly offered anywhere from $250 to $1000 to act as a "consultant" for a new psychiatric medication, which means that I am paid to sit in a room and listen to another doctor tout the remarkable effects of the company's new pill.

The pharmaceutical industry's influence over what research gets funded and even what research gets published has alarmed the guardians of medical academic integrity. Several class-action lawsuits have been filed by a consortium of law firms, alleging a conspiracy between the makers of Ritalin and organized American psychiatry to defraud the public. Although the claims may sound far-fetched on the surface, lawyers have learned (even without the aid of discovery) that the landmark meetings held by the American Psychiatric Association in the 1970s to change and greatly broaden the criteria for ADHD were funded almost entirely by the Novartis corporation, the makers of Ritalin. This financial support was not disclosed in either the resulting *Diagnostic and Statistical Manual* or the multitude of meetings held subsequently with professionals to educate them on the new criteria.

The law firms that have banded together in these suits are attacking what they see as a "social bad"—a situation in which industry, academia, government regulatory agencies, politicians, and even self-help groups are all walking in lockstep, even as children receive unproven medication. The trial lawyers—who won more than $1 billion in legal fees in the tobacco suit settlements—have said in public that they are prepared to pursue these cases, even if they first lose a hundred times in court, just as they did with tobacco, lead, and asbestos. And indeed, the first several suits have been dismissed. It seems tragic but inevitable that the issue of psychiatric drugs in children will ultimately be resolved by big business, lawyers, and the courts.

Stimulants and Selective Serotonin Reuptake Inhibitors: The Most Widely Prescribed Drug Classes

Stimulants

What They Do. These medications include the wildly popular Ritalin, Adderall, and Concerta, among other brands. They improve focus and concentration. And when used properly for ADHD-like symptoms of impulsivity, hyperactivity, and attention problems, they are highly effective. Studies show that stimulants have a 60-90 percent success rate; from my own experience, I would estimate that success closer to 90 percent.

Children who are impulsive and hyper may improve within *minutes* of taking an appropriate dose. I saw Tony, the truly hyperactive boy described in Chapter 7, two weeks after I had prescribed Ritalin. He took a ten-milligram dose two hours before the meeting. In sharp contrast to his previously fidgety state, he sat comfortably on the couch with his hands on his lap. His voice was steadier, and as I was talking to his mother, he actually raised his hand to make a comment! He was able to follow the conversation; later, he played quietly by himself with Legos. Yet he did not seem drugged or "zombified"—just more like a normal kid.

Other children who are not hyperactive or impulsive may take the drug to assist with work completion. They also benefit rapidly, although it sometimes takes two or three weeks until there is enough completed work for adults to notice the difference.

Stimulants get their name because in higher doses they increase blood pressure, heart rate, and alertness. They are not the kind of drugs you would initially expect to help hyper kids, and in fact there's a popular myth that stimulants have a paradoxical effect on children with ADHD. Normal children and adults, the myth goes, will experience increased activity and agitation on stimulants, whereas kids with ADHD will actually calm down. In reality, stimulants *in low doses* improve the ability of everyone—whether normal, impulsive, adult, or child—to stick with tasks that are boring and difficult. Hyperactive children may appear calmer simply because they are more methodical and more able to focus when they are taking the drugs. Although stimulants will not remediate a learning disability, they can help kids hang in there with assignments they find frustrating or dull.

Safety.   Stimulants have been used for symptoms of hyperactivity and impulsivity in children since 1937, and I've been using them in my own practice for more than twenty years. Stimulants have been examined more extensively than any other drug used in children; thousands of studies demonstrate their relative effectiveness and safety in the short term. One reason I like them is that they take effect swiftly—within minutes, as already noted—and then exit the bloodstream a few hours later (exactly how many hours later depends on the specific preparation). If there are troublesome side effects, they vanish quickly.

Thanks to this combination of pharmaceutical knowledge, history, and personal experience, I am much less hesitant to prescribe stimulants for kids than other drugs. If a child's problems persist after I've worked with the parents and school on establishing good behavioral and learning programs, or if the child, like Tony, exhibits an unusual degree of hyperactivity, I am likely to offer a stimulant medication.

But stimulants have not been examined with as much rigor as I or most concerned parents would like. Most studies have followed children for no more than a few weeks or months, and nearly all of them have focused on boys aged six to thirteen. I would like to see more studies cover longer periods of stimulant use, examine children years after they finish taking the drugs, and look at groups other than school-age boys. I also wish for studies that measure a child's improvement not just by a decrease in hyperactivity but by quality of life. Sure, kids on stimulants might fidget less—but do they have a better chance of finishing high school and avoiding drug abuse and trouble with the law than those who don't?

Choosing a Stimulant.   Most of the brand-name stimulants used for psychiatric conditions are versions of either amphetamine or methylphenidate, which is a synthetic derivative of amphetamine and nearly identical in chemical structure and function. Ritalin, Concerta, Metadate, and Methyllin contain methylphenidate as their active ingredient; Dexedrine, Dextrostat, and Adderall contain amphetamine.

Large-scale studies have shown no difference between the effectiveness, safety, and side effects of methylphenidate-based drugs versus those with amphetamine as their active ingredient. My own feeling, shared by other doctors, is that the amphetamine-based products are slightly more powerful and produce a few more side effects; however, many of my patients take amphetamine drugs without any problems at all. If one kind of drug does not work for your child's acting-out problems or produces intolerable side effects, it's certainly worth trying the other before going on to another nonstimulant class of drugs altogether. The other drug classes have their own—and potentially more serious—side effects and have not been studied as well in children.

Another factor to consider in choosing a stimulant is its length of action. Ritalin and a few others last about three to four hours, often a good length of time for kids in elementary school. The assistance they receive in focus and attention during the morning hours is sufficient to meet the major demands of their day; most important school work is done in the morning, with projects and fun activities frequently occupying the afternoon. I might add that the improved emotional state coming from their relative morning success probably carries these children through the afternoon and evening. Happy, satisfied children (even those with ADHD symptoms) can focus and delay their gratification better than unhappy, angry ones.

Until a few years ago, kids who needed more assistance from stimulants had to line up during lunchtime at the nurse's or school secretary's office for their second dose of Ritalin. These queues, along with the hassle and social stigma attached to them, are disappearing, thanks to the longer-acting drugs now on the market. Middle- and high-school-age young people, as well as younger children who are more severely affected by their problems, are candidates for preparations like Metadate ER, which lasts for six to eight hours, or Concerta, which lasts for about twelve. As well as being more convenient, these drugs reduce the possibility of the up-down-up experience, as the drug's effects wear off before the next dose begins to work. However, the longer-acting preparations are more likely to create sleep and appetite disturbances, which will be discussed shortly.

Why You May Need to Be Less Worried About Side Effects Than You Thought. Most children are able to tolerate stimulant medications without much trouble, and side effects can often be managed with commonsense measures. One of the most frequent problems is decreased appetite while the dose is at work. Kids who take a single morning dose of a short-acting preparation will usually see the return of their appetite by midday, but those who take longer-acting stimulants may not find lunch appealing. Most children do not seem to mind this effect, but a few are so bothered that it is worth lowering the dose or trying another medication altogether. When lunchtime appetites are curbed, parents and day care providers should be prepared to serve a big snack after school.

If a medication lasts through the early evening, kids may have trouble falling asleep. If insomnia occurs early in the dosing trial, I may urge the family to give the medication a few more days, since the problem will often fade on its own. If it does not, I usually either decrease the final dose or shift it to a time earlier in the day. Some doctors will add another drug on top of the stimulant to help the child fall asleep, but I am less enthusiastic about this option.

Although decreased appetite and trouble sleeping are the most common side effects, you may have also heard reports of other problems: headache, stomachache, rebound, tics, and growth delay. Most of these effects have not been consistently confirmed by recent studies. Headache and stomachache surface as complaints with about the same frequency when kids are given a placebo—apparently, for some kids the simple act of taking a pill increases anxiety, which leads to symptoms. These pains tend to go away once the children get used to taking the medication; until then, Tylenol relieves the headaches.

Irritability, known as "rebound," has not been well studied (it does not appear on manufacturers' lists of possible side effects). I join many other doctors in wondering if rebound is related less to drugs than to the witching hours of five and six o'clock in the evening, when medication is wearing off and parents, either exhausted from their workday or low on patience, must still deal with demanding and tired children. That doesn't mean I don't take rebound seriously. If it occurs, I first try to address it behaviorally, with the usual program of immediate and consistent rewards and punishments. If that strategy does not work, I may consider adding another dose of a short-acting stimulant late in the afternoon, one that permits an appetite for dinner and does not interfere with sleep. Some doctors like to add a sedating drug at this point, but I would rather try to find a single drug that works well enough rather than prescribe two drugs intended to balance each other out.

Until the late 1990s, doctors were concerned that stimulants could cause tics—involuntary muscle twitches or jerks—to develop in susceptible children. The connection has been closely examined in recent years and has not held up in the newest studies. When tics do emerge in kids taking stimulants, it is uncertain whether the drugs are to blame; perhaps the tics would have appeared anyway. Doctors and parents tend to agree that if the stimulant medication is helping, it's worth continuing even in the presence of tics. The involuntary movements wax and wane on their own and are not in themselves dangerous. But both parties should watch out for a negative social reaction, which could have a deleterious effect on the child's self-image. If tics do become troublesome, the parents and doctor should first try discontinuing the medication. If the tics continue, there is separate medication to address them.

Recent research has quieted another concern from the past—that stimulants decrease children's ultimate height. Although I have occasionally seen children lose some weight on the medication, especially initially, I cannot recall a youngster in my practice who had to stop stimulant medication because of persistent weight loss or failure to grow. Recent studies have shown that children with ADHD symptoms who take stimulants may achieve their final adult height later than non-ADHD kids, but the phenomenon is thought to be a result of their condition, not of taking stimulants.

Finally, some professionals and laypeople believe that if a child "has" bipolar disorder but has been misdiagnosed with ADHD, treatment with stimulants can potentiate (bring out) the more severe bipolar symptoms. But I find this reasoning specious—similar to arguing that drinking milk leads to heroin use because all heroin users first drank milk. Kids who develop more serious behavior symptoms while taking a stimulant are probably those who are facing bigger problems in the first place. I do *not* advocate the practice of skipping over the stimulant and moving directly to antipsychotics or anticonvulsants when bipolar disorder is suspected. Both classes of drugs carry far more risk and potential side effects.

What Parents Should Know About Dosing.   Typically, children are started on the lowest dose available of the chosen preparation, with a slightly higher dose given after every three to four days for a total of ten to fifteen days in all. During the trial period, I send a formal questionnaire to the teacher to aid me in determining the best dose (see page 159). I also ask parents to give the medication every day, even when they are planning eventually to use it only on school days, so that they can see the full effects of the medication on their child.

Watch out for the common therapeutic error of halting the dosage at the moment the child demonstrates any improvement. Unless the child is experiencing immediate side effects, there is no evidence that higher and more frequent doses of stimulants are any more dangerous than a low dose given only once a day. I strongly prefer to increase the dose until the optimal dosage—the one that produces the most improvement with the fewest side effects—is ascertained, on the theory that if a family is going to use medication, they ought to use it to its greatest effectiveness.

On the other hand, there is a point past which it rarely makes sense to continue increasing the dose. If a child has tried a twenty-milligram dose without effect, it's usually best to try another stimulant (perhaps an amphetamine-based drug if a methylphenidate product has failed, or vice versa) or, if needed, another drug class altogether.

Can My Child Take Less Medication on Weekends or More for a Special Event? Parents often worry that the stimulant must be taken continuously to have its proper effect. It does not. Most families do not give their kids stimulant medication when there isn't a clear demand on their performance or when their behavior isn't a problem. Weekends, vacations, and the summer months often mean no medication. I've noticed that the drop-off in visits to my Web site, www.docdiller.com, coincides with a decrease in the national sales of Ritalin in June. (Both return to the usual levels in September with the start of school.) There's no danger if, when planned, children don't take their medication. They simply don't concentrate or focus as well. I have no problem with families who wish to give their kids "drug vacations." Why take a drug every day if it isn't needed?

Should a child who normally takes stimulants only on school days receive an extra dose for a special event, like participating in a wedding or studying for an exam on Sunday afternoon? There is no risk of physical harm in this kind of occasional use, but I am wary of increasing the child's risk—or, more to the point, the parents' risk—of psychological dependence ("I need/He needs the drug to be successful"). Still, I can understand why a family might choose to use medication in these circumstances. More troubling is the older student who procrastinates and uses the medication only before an all-night cram session. I do not support such use because I believe it tolerates or promotes an irresponsible lifestyle.

What About Drug Abuse?   Perhaps the greatest lingering fear that parents have about stimulants is the question of drug abuse, since nearly all stimulant medications can be used to get high. (In fact, stimulants are not available in child-friendly suspensions because of concern that addicts could inject a liquid form of the drug. It's unlikely that the pharmaceutical industry will ever risk the possibility of adverse publicity that would attend such abuse.) But I rarely worry about stimulant abuse in preteens. They do not report a high on oral doses and complain about feeling nervous or jittery on too large a dose. Also, it is easy for parents to control access to the drug. No preteen in my practice, to my knowledge, has abused Ritalin.

Teens are another story. One study claims to prove that stimulants used in childhood increase the risk of teenage drug abuse later when compared with children who did not take stimulants, but the children studied were not randomly assigned to the medication or nonmedication groups. It's possible that the children who took the medication had more severe behavior problems to begin with and were therefore more prone to abuse in the first place. Nor do I take comfort from another study concluding that teens who take stimulants prescribed by a doctor are, ironically, somehow "protected" from taking illegal drugs. Again, I felt that the kids and families who were willing to take the medication constituted a different kind of group from those who chose not to.

In general, I think that when stimulants prescribed by a doctor are taken as directed (orally, not snorted), the chances of teen stimulant abuse are very, very small. It's my belief that kids with significant problems who wind up taking stimulants prescribed to them are, because of their own personalities and lifestyles, simply more likely to try and abuse drugs, alcohol, and cigarettes. If stimulants produce a "presensitizing" effect toward later abuse of drugs, I feel it is quite limited. I suspect that positive family relationships are the most protective element against drug abuse in the long term.

That said, the reports of increasing prescription stimulant abuse in high schools and on college campuses are alarming. So are media stories of kids getting hooked on Ritalin. Before receiving a stimulant, teens should be screened for personal and family histories of drug problems and for their overall level of responsibility. Those with very erratic behavior may simply not be candidates for this particular drug class.

When I prescribe stimulants for teens, I tell parents that these medications are not the kind that you can leave out on the kitchen table. I feel strongly that even the most mature teens should not have free access to the medication. Although they themselves may not abuse the drug, they may feel pressure from their peers to give away or to sell their pills. (In the course of twenty years, three families in my practice have reported a missing bottle of stimulants. They were each given one more chance, and all managed to guard the medication successfully after the reported loss.)

Do Stimulants Solve the Problem?   Although I am fairly comfortable prescribing stimulants, provided that the family and school are doing their part too, I am not convinced that they lead to long-term improvement. The few studies that have followed kids on stimulants beyond adolescence did *not* show fewer instances of dropping out or getting into trouble with the law. One long-term study of Ritalin showed that although the drugs were helpful, family counseling and special education were more important. Just like the drug-abuse studies, however, this study has been criticized for not randomly selecting families to one treatment or another. In other words, the kids and families who chose or stuck with family counseling may have differed from those who wanted medication only.

According to some dramatic headlines in professional journals as well as the general press, the most recent long-term study (which lasted about fourteen months) showed an opposite result—that symptoms improved most with medication. In the Multimodal Treatment for ADHD (MTA) study of some six hundred children, psychosocial interventions alone did not have as powerful an effect as the medication alone. However, with more time and more analysis, even this study seemed to indicate that for many of the problems that coexist with ADHD symptoms, such as learning difficulties, opposition, and anxiety, behavioral interventions were important. Most leading researchers remain uneasy with a message that says "stimulants only."

Prozac and Friends: Selective Serotonin Reuptake Inhibitors (SSRIs)

A Short History of SSRIs.   More than any other drug, Prozac is responsible for revolutionizing American psychiatry and the public's ideas about behavior and personality. Eli Lilly released Prozac in 1988, after years of systematic research into compounds that might affect the release of serotonin, a neurotransmitter thought to be a possible mediator in depression. Eventually, its scientists discovered fluoxetin, the generic name for Prozac, which selectively increases the amount of serotonin available to nerve cells. Today, Prozac is only one of several drugs, including the popular Paxil and Zoloft, in the class of selective serotonin reuptake inhibitors, or SSRIs.

Drugs for treating depression had been around for decades before Prozac burst onto the scene, but their side effects, including sedation, could be so unpleasant that doctors and their patients turned to them only in severe cases. Even then, the older antidepressants were doled out with extreme caution, as they could be fatal in large quantities and became a leading means of suicide among the deeply depressed. But Prozac appeared to be quite safe in early trials. It became attractive not just to people who fit the DSM criteria for depression but to the "walking wounded"—those who felt low or blue. Now, despite news of more serious side effects, the drugs are used for a host of problems aside from depression: obsessive-compulsion, anxiety, and panic disorders, agoraphobia, bulimia, and posttraumatic stress disorder, just to name a few. Our collective experience with the drug—about one in ten Americans has tried an SSRI—has made us much more comfortable with biochemical explanations of mood as well as biochemical means of adjusting it.

Are SSRIs Effective for Kids? In adults, one reason so many different problems get better with SSRIs is that they have a nonspecific effect on mood—they appear to decrease sensitivity to emotional insult and pain. While the mood-elevating qualities of SSRIs are quite helpful with the depressed patient, the increased resilience is an aid to whatever ails adults emotionally.

But it's far too early to conclude that these effects extend to kids as well as to adults. Of the SSRIs, only two—Paxil and Luvox—have proved effective for pediatric obsessive-compulsive disorder in the clinical trials required by the FDA. No other SSRI, as yet, has met FDA approval for pediatric use, nor have Paxil and Luvox been approved for use in childhood problems other than OCD. As of this writing, only seven or eight controlled, systematic studies have looked at the effects of SSRIs in children, and only one of those studies followed the children for as long as a year. One uncontrolled, nonblinded study (which leaves open the possibility of a huge placebo effect) found Prozac helpful in irritable children, probably because it decreased their sensitivity. Although I do not generally use SSRIs for younger children in my own practice, I do see a number of teens who are on the drugs. They choose to continue to take them out of a sense that the medications have been helpful. But they do not speak of the dramatic turnarounds that adults report on SSRIs.

Despite the dearth of good evidence, SSRIs have been prescribed to an estimated 1.5 million children under the age of eighteen. The majority of these kids are adolescents, girls especially, but children as young as two have been given Prozac. I am not alone in worrying that our current use of these drugs in so many children is not supported by enough research.

Side Effects and Safety.   Unlike the stimulants, which exit the bloodstream within hours, it may take one or two months before the body entirely eliminates an SSRI. Bear this in mind as you consider the possible side effects, since a bad reaction could stick around for a while.

Of all the known side effects, sleep disturbances are the most common. They often fade away within a few days after the drug is begun; if they do not, the doctor may decrease the dosage, divide the dosages throughout the day, or try a different SSRI. Some doctors add a sleep agent or an antihistamine like Benadryl, but, as I have already indicated, I try to get by with the fewest medications possible. Paxil and Luvox are less stimulatory and may be an option for patients with trouble sleeping; some doctors even prescribe them for anxious children to take in the evening.

This mild stimulatory quality of SSRIs occasionally has more potent effects on individual children. One fourteen-year-old patient of mine, Mark, had taken Prozac for a week when he became violent in my waiting room. His father and I literally had to sit on him. He had never been so out of control before taking the drug, nor did the problem recur after I took him off it. Another patient, ten-year-old Claire, surprised me by coming into the office with a dozen of her pet salamanders creeping over her sweater. As she talked with me, she began to pick imaginary warts off the salamanders. I finally asked her to stop because I thought she was abusing the animals. She had been on Prozac for two months and had never before acted so strangely. I also discontinued her medication.

There is a small chance that an SSRI will affect the metabolism and action of other drugs. SSRIs can increase the blood level of other antidepressants and theoretically affect the breakdown of some antihistamines. If your child takes an SSRI, you should check with the doctor regarding interactions with other medications.

From what I have seen in my practice, from anecdotal evidence, and from the very limited research, SSRIs seem generally well tolerated by children. But it's not the risk of known side effects that worries me. It's the risk of *unknown* ones. Prozac and the other SSRIs have only been around for fourteen years, and it's only in the last five years or so that they've been used in large numbers of children. We simply don't know if an important untoward consequence will surface in the future. Even now, there have been some rare reports linking Prozac to tardive dyskinesias—involuntary and permanent muscle movement problems that in the past have been mainly associated with major antipsychotic drugs like Thorazine or Mellaril. Granted, these cases are highly unusual, given the millions of people who have taken the drug.

Another disturbing but often ignored possibility is sexual side effects. About one in three adults who take SSRIs will experience sexual problems, including difficulty reaching orgasm, impotence, and decreased libido. One wouldn't think that these effects should pose a problem for children who are not sexually active—but tell that to the fourteen-year-old boy taking Zoloft, who in panic confided to his father that he could no longer ejaculate or achieve orgasm while masturbating. No one told him that this was a common side effect of SSRIs among adult men. And I am uneasy about the long-term effects of drugs known to affect sexuality on the developing brains of young children and adolescents.

If My Child Is Going to Take an SSRI, What Kind Is Best?   There is not a great deal of difference among the SSRIs. Prozac is the most stimulatory (possibly helpful with depression), while Paxil and

Luvox are more sedating, which may be useful with anxiety. Your doctor may have a preference, and family members who have tried SSRIs can suggest a specific drug to try or avoid, depending on their responses.

Like stimulants, SSRIs vary in their length of action. Prozac can take as long as a month to build up to consistent levels in the body, and its effects can last for weeks, making it ideal for busy parents who may forget to give the medication or for teens who don't always remember to take it. All the other SSRI drugs have a faster build-up time and last about twenty-four hours. If a child or parent is especially worried about potential side effects, I'm more likely to prescribe these preparations than Prozac. If any intolerable problems appear, the drug can be eliminated from the body more quickly.

Another consideration is the form of the drug. Prozac, Paxil, and Celexa are now available in a liquid form, which is useful for kids who can't swallow pills or whose parents need to use a medicine dropper to dole out very precise and small amounts.

When Does an SSRI Make Sense?　It would certainly be nice to have more data on these drugs. I'd especially like to see a study that follows a group of children on SSRIs into postadolescence, to see if the medications made a difference in their lives or if any serious side effects developed. But these kinds of trials are very difficult to run and maintain, so I'm not holding my breath. In the meantime, is it right to avoid SSRIs when a child is suffering?

My temporary solution has been to adjust my scales. Because there is much less evidence of the effectiveness and safety of SSRIs compared to stimulants, a significantly higher degree of compromised function or disability must be present in order to offset the uncertainties. Threats of suicide or actual attempts, especially in teens, often lead me to offer medication at the beginning of a treatment. Refusal to go to school or to leave the house severely compromises the life of a child and may call for a medication intervention. (Even though one early study failed to show benefits of SSRIs for these specific problems, I might use one in a "fishing expedition," hoping that the drug will improve the child's mood or resilience.)

If a sixteen-year-old girl, showing many signs of depression, is talking about taking her life, I will likely offer her an SSRI. But if a fear of spiders is keeping a seven-year-old girl from going to the playground, I will strongly commit to working with her and her parents before I prescribe one of these drugs. I may also consider SSRIs for kids with serious relatedness problems, ones whose tantrums or odd behaviors are thought to be connected to anxiety. But again, the evidence is weak. Unfortunately for the million and a half kids currently taking SSRIs in America, *they* are the experiment, the results of which I am anxiously awaiting.

Other Pharmaceutical Options

Antipsychotics

Why They Are Used.   The antipsychotic drugs, so named because they were initially tested for symptoms of schizophrenia, are employed for extremely difficult behavior problems, especially in kids classified as "bipolar." These drugs are used to decrease anxiety and agitation, reduce aggressive behavior, and diminish the symptoms of psychosis (including visual and auditory hallucinations and disordered thinking). Some are also used to reduce involuntary tics.

Effectiveness in Children.   A few short-term studies claim to show that antipsychotics improve aggression in hospitalized adolescents, and a recent journal article showed that low doses of one antipsychotic, Risperdal, controlled aggressive behavior in autistic and retarded preteens. But none of these studies lasted longer than a few weeks, and none of them was double-blinded with placebo control.

However, there *is* good evidence that low doses of some antipsychotics, including Haldol, decrease the frequency of tics.

Side Effects.   Serious side effects make antipsychotics something of a Faustian bargain, fraught with long-term implications. Sedation is a side effect common to all the antipsychotic medications, as are increased appetite and significant weight gain. (The chief child psychiatrist at Langley Porter, the psychiatric hospital of the University of California–San Francisco, has described the weight gain of some kids as "Pickwickian," a Dickensian term used to describe people so overweight that their breathing is compromised. I'm not sure that the children were quite that obese, but they suffered serious cosmetic alterations.) Muscle tightness and spasm, a major sense of restlessness, and a Parkinson's disease-like condition, with tremor, general slowness, and flat facial affect are not uncommon with long-term use. The older versions of antipsychotics can also lead to dry mouth, blurred vision, constipation, and increased heart rate (without apparent danger). Depending on the side effect, changes in dosage and scheduling or switching to another medication can reduce the problems. Sometimes either Benadryl or Cogentin (amantidine) is prescribed with an antipsychotic to decrease the likelihood of side effects developing.

Two complications of antipsychotics are especially dreaded. The first, neuroleptic malignant syndrome, in which the patient experiences muscle spasms, confusion, and high fever, mandates immediate hospitalization. There can be serious, even fatal, kidney damage in this very rare illness. The other, a permanent muscle movement disorder called tardive dyskinesia, is much more common and insidious. Usually the first signs are involuntary facial movements like lip smacking, tongue rolling, eye blinks, and grimaces. Over time, larger muscle groups of the trunk and limbs can be affected. Most of us have seen chronic ex-psychiatric hospital patients, now homeless, exhibiting these symptoms. Sometimes they go away when the drug is discontinued, but not always. This side effect is more common when a child takes higher doses or when the drug is prescribed for a long period of time. (Oddly enough, when antipsychotics like Haldol are used to *treat* tics, they very rarely produce additional involuntary movements.)

Choosing an Antipsychotic.   Most doctors today, given their choice, will prescribe the newer generation of antipsychotics, which includes the brand names Risperdal and Zyprexa. These drugs, the so-called novel or atypical antipsychotics, are supposedly better tolerated in the short term and are claimed to produce fewer instances of tardive dyskinesia (unwanted movements). I'll be more enthusiastic about these claims when the drugs have been around longer. For now, it's quite possible that they have fewer known side effects simply because they have not been studied as thoroughly as the older drugs.

The old-line brands like Mellaril and Haldol may still be used on occasion, especially in state and county hospitals where their cheaper cost is a deciding factor. Haldol is more commonly used as a second-line drug for tics.

When Do Antipsychotics Make Sense?   I am deeply wary of the growing acceptance of antipsychotics for kids. Over 200,000 children receive antipsychotic medications, mostly to control unruly behavior rather than to treat hallucinations or other symptoms of serious psychosis. This explosive growth of prescriptions is driven partly by the allegedly superior and safer new drugs (as well as by the popularity of the controversial bipolar diagnosis, discussed elsewhere in this book). But I try to keep in mind the "five-year rule" of psychiatric medications; who knows what will turn up as more reports of these drugs come in? Antipsychotics, like anticonvulsants and lithium, are desperate and potentially dangerous interventions for kids perceived to be in desperate and dangerous straits.

When used for a few weeks to manage a crisis, antipsychotics may allow for recovery and hope. But the future is gloomy for children who remain on these drugs for months and years. Many of these kids have had institutional experiences (foster care, group homes, psychiatric hospitals, and special schools). Many of them come from single-parent, no-parent, or broken homes; often they have experienced poverty, abuse, racism, and parental substance abuse. They were likely born with vulnerable and difficult personalities, learning problems, or mental retardation. Almost all of these kids are damaged and are victims. They could have avoided their fate only with a nearly impossible-to-deliver environment of stable parents and spectacular schools. Most will continue to have serious problems throughout life, unless they are lucky enough to find an environment that meets their profoundly great needs.

Anticonvulsants

Why They Are Used.   As their name implies, the anticonvulsant drugs were first developed and tested to control seizures and epilepsy. As psychiatric medicines, they are used to "take the edge off" angry and oppositional behavior, especially the severe kind that is being categorized as "bipolar disorder."

Effectiveness in Children.   Studies on the efficacy and safety of these drugs for kids with psychiatric problems is minimal to nonexistent. As of this writing, a consensus is developing among doctors that the newer antipsychotic drugs work better for the same problems. Nevertheless, anticonvulsants are used regularly when other psychoactive medications have failed; today, hundreds of thousands of children are taking anticonvulsants for emotional or behavior problems, usually in combination with other psychiatric drugs.

Side Effects.   If one of your grandparents or an elderly relative took anticonvulsants for epilepsy, you may recall the drug's heavily sedating quality. You should know that in the past couple of decades, preparations have been introduced that cause much less sedation (and produce fewer other side effects) than the old-line drugs of decades past. However, all anticonvulsants, no matter how new, can cause sleepiness and decreased mental acuity; they work by suppressing brain activity. All the adult patients or friends I know who currently take an anticonvulsant for a seizure disorder have told me they would prefer to be off the medication if it were possible—the sedation and subtle effects on cognition are that disturbing. Children who take them may fall asleep in the middle of the school day, encounter new difficulties with schoolwork, or decide to nap instead of playing at home.

Other side effects vary according to the drug used; a more detailed list of anticonvulsants can be found in the guide at the back of this book. Depakote, the most popular anticonvulsant for behavior problems, can lead to dizziness as well as weight gain or loss. More serious potential side effects include reductions in white blood cells, which if not caught in time can lead to fatal leukemia or aplastic anemia and infections. The medication can also cause hepatitis, although this inflammation of the liver appears to be reversible if the drug is stopped. As a precaution against both of these possibilities, your child will need blood tests before starting the drug and every six months while taking it. Ovarian cysts and polycystic ovaries in young women taking the drug for seizure control have been reported. Recently the manufacturer of Depakote was forced by the FDA to send a letter to physicians alerting them to reports of hemorrhagic pancreatitis (a severe gastrointestinal condition that is sometimes fatal) associated with the drug.

Because of Depakote's potentially lethal complications, as well as growing word-of-mouth skepticism among doctors over its effectiveness in treating children's behavior problems, many physicians are now choosing Neurontin instead. Neurontin, which is newer than Depakote, causes dizziness but apparently less sedation. As yet, no blood tests are required for kids on Neurontin, nor have any lethal side effects been reported in children. But keep in mind that this low side effect profile may simply reflect a lack of experience with the drug. No long-term studies have been conducted that can tell doctors and parents whether any side effects comparable to those of Depakote and other anticovulsants will emerge.

When Do Anticonvulsants Make Sense?   I rarely prescribe anticonvulsants; as with antipsychotics, I reserve them for desperate situations. If I am considering these drugs, the parents and I are usually facing other tough questions simultaneously: Should the child be moved to a special day class? Can the child live at home, or is a special boarding school a better idea? Are there threats of physical harm, either to the child or to others? Should the parents consider separating because of ongoing and severe marital problems?

Lithium

Why It Is Used.   In the 1950s, lithium was found to be helpful in treating and preventing bouts of manic-depressive disorder in adults. Several excellent short- and long-term studies *on adults* established that in most cases, lithium's positive effects outweighed its sometimes difficult ones. Lithium's efficacy has come into question in recent years, but that may be thanks to the ever broadening category of people considered candidates for its use. Although lithium is not as popular as the anticonvulsants or antipsychotics, it has started to come up regularly as a choice for very difficult children.

Effectiveness.   Despite the good evidence for lithium in adults, there are no studies that demonstrate its efficacy for childhood behavior problems.

Side Effects.   Lithium is not an easy drug for children to take, and parents and doctors must be prepared for the work of managing it successfully. Side effects are numerous and fairly common. They include nausea, vomiting, stomach pain, tremors, sedation, and increased urination and thirst. Kidney function can be affected and damaged, so children on lithium must drink water frequently; if they catch a stomach flu, they will need to be watched for dehydration. Long-term use of lithium may also cause hypothyroidism. Children who take the drug need to give blood samples before starting the medication and every six months thereafter. Severe acne eruptions while on lithium discourage teens, especially, from continuing its use.

Since lithium can interact with other medications, including some over-the-counter anti-inflammatory drugs like Advil, you'll need to check with the doctor before giving your child any other medications. Ironically, lithium is rarely prescribed alone to children; most kids will be taking at least one other psychiatric medication.

When Does Lithium Make Sense?   Lithium is a serious and potentially dangerous drug. It is not one to be considered lightly. I believe its use should be reserved for the same kinds of situations appropriate for antipsychotics (discussed above).

Tricyclics

Why They Are Used.   These medications include imipramine, desipramine, nortriptyline, Elavil, and Anafranil. Tricyclics were first discovered to be of value in treating adult depression in the 1950s, and they are among the oldest psychotropic agents still being used by doctors today. Although they were found ineffective in managing depressive symptoms in childhood, they are currently used as a second or third line for children's anxiety problems when other medications have failed. They may also be considered for serious acting-out behaviors when stimulants have not been successful.

Effectiveness. I've already mentioned that the tricyclics were studied for the treatment of childhood depression decades ago and found to be ineffective. But now, with an expanding definition of what constitutes "depression" in childhood, along with a general openness toward more aggressive use of psychiatric drugs in children, the tricyclics have made something of a comeback, usually for symptoms that lean more toward anxiety than depression.

Side Effects. The side effects make these drugs difficult for many kids to take. Imagine the drowsiness and dry mouth that accompany most over-the-counter cold preparations; multiply that times ten and you get close to the experience of the tricyclics' side effects. Blurred vision and constipation are other common problems. There are no clear long-term side effects, but stopping the medications suddenly (as opposed to tapering off gradually) can produce a mild withdrawal reaction of headache, stomachache, vomiting, and diarrhea. If there is any chance that a child or someone in the family may intentionally overdose, tricyclics are a very risky option, since in large quantities they are a sure-fire means of suicide.

In the 1990s, tricyclics were vigorously promoted as a second-line medication for the treatment of ADHD symptoms, but the sudden deaths of several children who were taking them soon cast a pall over that trend. None of the children overdosed on the medication; some of them were involved in vigorous exercise during or just before their sudden collapse and death. Children are now recommended to have an electrocardiogram (EKG) before beginning tricyclics to rule out any undetected congenital abnormality in their heart's rhythm. Often, another EKG is obtained after ascertaining the optimal dose, to make certain there have been no important changes to the cardiac rhythm. However, it is not clear at all whether screening for predisposing cardiac problems or monitoring the heartbeat in any way protects children who take these drugs from an admittedly rare but catastrophic event.

Which Tricyclic Is Best?   Tricyclics come in a variety of preparations; often, the factor that determines which drug is chosen is the extent of its sedating effect. If it's useful to bring on sleep in the evening, a more sedating drug, like Elavil or Anafranil, may be used. If sedation is to be avoided as much as possible, the doctor may prescribe desipramine.

When Do Tricyclics Make Sense?   Considering the evidence that tricylics are *not* useful for depressive symptoms in childhood, along with the reports of deaths, I am uneasy with their use. They should be considered only when a child's function is seriously impaired and when both behavioral interventions and other drugs have failed. I would be deeply concerned about giving a tricyclic to a teen who is talking about suicide.

Clonidine and Tenex: Antihypertensives

Clonidine (also known by the brand name Catapres) is the best example of a drug that was systematically tested in fewer than one hundred children for the treatment of psychiatric problems but has been prescribed to hundreds of thousands of kids in America. Clonidine, along with the similar-acting drug Tenex (guanafacine), is most often used as an adjunct medication for dealing with late afternoon/early evening acting-out problems when another dose of stimulant medication cannot be given because appetite for dinner and sleep will be affected. Clonidine and Tenex are also used as a first-line drug intervention for the treatment of Tourette's syndrome.

Effectiveness.   I'm not overwhelmed with the evidence for the behavioral effects of these drugs. They produce mild sedation, which might be helpful in a few cases for the afternoons and evenings. For

Tourette's I think that clonidine and Tenex are reasonable drugs. They are better tolerated than the antipsychotic Haldol (also used for this condition) but, in my opinion, are not as effective.

Side Effects.   The main side effect of both clonidine and Tenex is sedation, which makes it a popular choice as a late-in-the-day intervention but can be problematic for full-day use. When it is given to control Tourette's, finding the right balance between complete cessation of tics and oversedation often means that some breakthrough of tic behavior occurs.

Although the antihypertensives were originally developed for reduction and control of high blood pressure in adults, they rarely affect blood pressure in the doses given to children for behavioral problems. However, any dizziness and fainting that occur when abruptly getting up from a lying position (called postural hypotension) is an early sign of too much medication. Parents should know that neither clonidine nor Tenex should be stopped abruptly, because of a mostly theoretical risk of a sudden rise in blood pressure, which can cause headache and the remote possibility of a cerebral stroke.

Several children have died while taking clonidine in combination with other psychiatric drugs, which calls into question the safety of this category of medicine for use in children's behavior problems. The connection between the development of cardiac arrhythmias and taking clonidine or Tenex is still speculative, although parents should be aware of the remote possibility. Pre- and postdrug electrocardiograms are recommended to screen for any cardiac danger signs.

Atypical Antidepressants

The loosely defined group of drugs known as "atypical antidepressants" was initially developed and tested for the treatment of adult depression. They are now widely used for an array of problems, mostly of the depressive or anxious variety. They are used with varying frequency in children, waxing and waning according to investigators' interest, drug company support, and reports of side effects. There are virtually no studies on either of these drugs in kids; the few that have been published are nonblinded.

Wellbutrin is most widely prescribed as a drug named Zyban, promoted as an aid to smoking cessation. No matter what the name, the drug's effectiveness is likely a result of increased resilience and decreased sensitivity. It also improves attention and focus to a limited degree, making it a second choice when stimulants have failed. My experience prescribing the drug suggests that it is neither as effective as the Prozac class in addressing depressive symptoms nor as effective as the stimulant class in treating the symptoms of ADHD. Still, if a teen shows signs of both depression and attention problems, Wellbutrin may be a reasonable choice. It may also be tried first if there are concerns about a teen possibly abusing a stimulant.

Wellbutrin has few known side effects, although irritability can occur with higher doses. Daily doses higher than 450 milligrams are associated with an increased risk of grand mal seizures.

Effexor is a new antidepressant drug that fits in somewhere between the SSRI class and the older tricyclics. Its purported action on the pathways of two neurotransmitters (serotonin and norepinephrine) has been hailed by its manufacturer as an advance in the treatment of depression. I cannot help but feel cynical about this promotional tactic. I remember when the drug companies first advertised Prozac and the other SSRIs to physicians. They were touted as "clean" antidepressants because they affected only *one* neurotransmitter pathway, serotonin, and therefore had fewer side effects than the older tricyclics, which affect multiple pathways. Ten years later the "dirty" actions of Effexor are highlighted *as an advantage*. The beat goes on . . . Nevertheless, Effexor has a limited place in childhood psychiatric medications, usually as a second- or third-choice medication for children who display acting-out behaviors and who are also felt to be anxious or depressed.

Trazodone was initially developed as an antidepressant but was far too sedating for most people. Instead, it has found a place in the drug armamentarium in low doses as a sleep-inducing agent. One unusual side effect of trazodone is priapism—a prolonged, generally painful erection of the penis. In extremely rare situations, priapism can be a medical emergency, in which the dilated blood vessels of the penis must be surgically relieved to prevent permanent damage.

Valium and Its Descendants: Antianxiety Drugs

What They Do.   Librium (chlordiazepoxide) and its better-known sister Valium were made famous and infamous in the 1950s and early 1960s as "mother's little helpers" and "dolls"—as in *Valley of the Dolls*, a novel about young women addicted to alcohol and prescription drugs. They and a long list of variations called the benzodiazepines are anxiolytic—they cut anxiety, generally via mild to moderate sedation. They are used in children primarily for sleep problems and major anxiety, usually as an adjunct to other drugs. The most popular antianxiety medications include not just Valium but Xanax, Ativan, and others.

Effectiveness.   There are few good studies on the effects of these drugs on children. They have been shown ineffective for phobias and separation anxieties in preteens, as they are simply too sedating at levels where they begin to suppress the anxious symptoms.

Side Effects.   All these drugs cause sedation, which make sense for nighttime sleep disturbances but obviously may be a hindrance to daytime use. Combining these drugs with alcohol—always a potential problem where teens are concerned—can lead to respiratory arrest and even death. Over time and with regular use, physical addiction and tolerance—the need for a higher and higher dose to achieve the same effect—can develop. The addiction is a difficult one to quit without hospitalization and the initial substitution of other drugs to replace the benzodiazepam. Nevertheless, many people take these drugs for short periods of time to help with anxiety or sleep, and some can continue at a steady dose for years without tolerance developing. I've never heard of a child experiencing major withdrawal problems from an antianxiety medication, but parents and doctors should be on heightened alert if a child who has been on the drug for some time requires a higher dose to receive the same effect.

Choosing a Drug.   These drugs differ primarily by how quickly they take effect and how long they last. Drugs like Ambien or Sonata, with fairly immediate and short-term effects, are used as sleeping agents. Klonopin lasts much longer and may be given twice a day for round-the-clock action. Xanax and Ativan are frequently prescribed because of their higher potency and medium duration of action. Pharmaceutical companies regularly introduce variations of these drugs and then promote them heavily, accentuating minor differences or touting fewer side effects. These drugs tend to follow the five-year rule, so you'll need to keep your wits about you as you sort through the constantly changing information. "New" drugs of this type very likely will make their appearance by the time you are reading this book.

Buspar (buspirone) is another relatively new antianxiety agent that differs from the Valium class of drugs in structure and action. It does not lead to tolerance and addiction and is said to have fewer side effects. Many doctors, however, wonder whether Buspar has any effects at all. It appears to be a weaker antianxiety medication but may still have a place in the treatment of milder problems.

When Do Antianxiety Drugs Make Sense?   Because in children sedation tends to occur at the doses at which the antianxiety effects begin,
I do not prescribe these agents much to kids. They can be useful,
often in combination with an SSRI, for stressed mothers and fathers
who have become depressed and anxious.

9

What If Your Child Can't Swallow the Pill? (And Other Questions About Day-to-Day Life with Psychiatric Drugs)

Parents considering psychoactive drugs as part of their child's treatment plan are often concerned about the practical challenges—whether to include the child in the decision, what to tell Aunt Jesse about the drug, and how to keep a medication log. In this chapter I give my responses to the questions parents ask most frequently.

What Do I Tell My Child About the Medication?

I encourage parents to tell the truth on a level that is appropriate to the child's age and understanding. The good intentions behind outright lies—such as telling the child that the pill is a vitamin—could boomerang if there are side effects or if the child doesn't attach any importance to taking the daily dose. Most of the time, a short explanation is best: "This pill is going to help you pay better attention/stick with your homework/help you think longer before you misbehave/ fight Mr. Anger."

Kids also need to know that responsibility for their behavior still resides with them, not the pill. A drug won't turn a "no" into a "yes." I usually emphasize this by explaining that the drug won't force them to do anything they don't want to do or magically make their hand push their pencil across a page of homework. "You'll still need to try on your own," I say. Avoid statements that rob the child of self-determination, for example, "this pill will make you good." (Frustrated parents once told their seven-year-old that he was coming to my office to "get his brain fixed." I'm not sure what he expected—neurosurgery?—but he seemed awfully relieved to see the bins of toys.)

When kids seem worried about taking a drug, I ask for specifics. Kids under eight are mostly concerned about the size and taste of the pill. Is it big? Is it hard to swallow?

Older children and teens (and a few from the younger set) often ask about side effects. Even when they don't voice concerns, the doctor or parents should explain the most common and immediate problems, such as not feeling an appetite for lunch or having trouble falling asleep (if the drug is a stimulant), or feeling drowsy during the day (for drugs with a sedative effect).

What If My Child Doesn't Want to Take the Drug?

The answer depends on the child's age and maturity. If a child under twelve doesn't want to take the pill, ask, "How come?"

Most kids don't want to take pills because they find them difficult to swallow without chewing; some kids try to avoid anything that's an extra responsibility or hassle. In these cases, parents can practice with their children to make swallowing easier (see the next question for more details) and offer rewards for taking the pills. Or they can just insist, in the same way they'd insist a child receive a vaccination.

Sometimes refusing drugs is part of a wider pattern of opposition (Dad says "black" and the child automatically says "white"). Taking the pill is just another battle over limits. In these cases, parents can, once again, insist: "Take it because I told you so."

Young children can also pick up on their parents' ambivalence about the medication; they can tell that taking Ritalin is different from taking amoxicillin for an ear infection. Parents should reassure children after exploring and validating their concerns. In the worst-case scenario, one parent is strongly against the medication but the other has prevailed—usually by force of will but sometimes through the court system. Here, taking the pill has become a symbolic act of disloyalty to the antidrug parent, and the child will be more likely not just to oppose the pill but to complain of side effects.

I strongly resist medicating a child when one parent is dead set against it. Any positive effect the drug might have is outweighed by making the child's actions a fulcrum for parental conflict. Instead, I continue to work with the parents in an attempt to forge some compromise, such as agreeing to a drug trial or to a drug-free period of two weeks with specific behavior and performance parameters.

Older kids may refuse drugs out of a concern over side effects. But some refuse medication as a point of developmental honor and independence. They may view taking a pill as a sign of their failure or difference. A more adult-like conversation is reasonable here, in which the parents and child (and possibly the doctor) sift through the pros and cons together. It may be advisable to give teenagers a clearly defined, drug-free trial in which to meet certain standards of behavior—say, two weeks of turning homework in on time and obeying parental rules. Teens will often accept pills if this trial doesn't work out.

Some teens, however, are locked in a conflict with their parents over their freedoms and right to choose for themselves—a conflict often heightened by a teen's demonstrations of irresponsibility—and experience rules as a call to rebellion. The irony for many families of rebellious teens is that by the time a child is willing to take medication, she no longer needs it, simply because she is now more agreeable, responsible, or mature. It is wise for parents to keep in mind that some studies showing positive results of heavy medication were performed on teens who were in psychiatric hospitals against their will; families at home are facing a very different set of circumstances. In most cases, I advise against ordering recalcitrant teenagers to take a drug—you run the risk of generating an antagonism that is worse than the pill's positive effects. In a few sad situations, however, parents may have to insist on medication if the child is to continue living at home.

What If My Child Can't Swallow the Pill?

Of the psychoactive drugs used in children, only a few are available in a nonpill form. Four SSRIs come in a liquid preparation, and clonidine is available in a skin patch. The American pharmaceutical industry, ever alert to consumer needs and potential marketing niches, is nearly finished with clinical testing of a skin patch that will deliver a steady, twelve-hour dose of stimulant medication. But most kids on medication will need to take pills.

Although swallowing pills is a pressing concern for both parents and children, *I have never had to take a child off medication because she couldn't get it down.* Sometimes a few accommodations do the trick. The drug can be put inside a minimarshmallow or—as long as the medication isn't long acting—crushed into yogurt or applesauce. When a drug must be swallowed whole, kids can practice with small tablets of flavored Tylenol. (One doctor is famous for having kids practice by swallowing edible cake toppings!) Parents can also give rewards for efforts to swallow.

Although Ritalin and many other stimulants come in pills that look small even to children, the newer, longer-acting drugs may pose more of a challenge. They must not be crushed (which destroys the time-release effect), and they tend to be larger. If a child cannot learn to swallow these bigger pills, the doctor may prescribe several smaller ones to be taken at the same time. But then the child has to make two or three efforts to swallow rather than just one.

What Do I Tell Relatives, Teachers, and My Other Kids?

Keeping the drug a secret from the child's siblings is not just difficult; it can inflate the act of taking a pill into a dramatic, big-deal event. Again, an honest approach is usually best: "Johnny will be taking a medicine to help him pay attention. This is private, just between us and the rest of the family, but it's not bad. You wouldn't tell your friends the color of Johnny's underwear, because that would be mean, right? So if you tell your friends about Johnny's pills, you'll be in trouble with me."

Whether to tell adults outside of the immediate family is a personal issue, but most parents want or need to tell others about the drug. A firm but nondefensive statement usually works: "We've tried a number of things so far, and we're still exploring our options. But we've decided to give medication a try to see if it will help."

Since school behavior and performance are often the driving factors behind medication, feedback from teachers during the drug trial is essential. It's possible to get a "blind" response by making a simple request: "Please pay attention to my son's work completion this week." But ultimately the teacher's curiosity may lead her to conclusions that are exaggerated or incorrect, so I would opt for a short version of the truth. A parent can mention the medication without getting into specifics.

How Do I Keep Track of My Child's Performance on the Drug?

In the initial phases of prescription, a record is invaluable. It helps you and the doctor determine the drug's effects—both desirable and unwanted—as well as the optimum dosage. At first, you should take daily notes of the dosage and frequency of each medication, along with its effects on behavior and physical well-being. I include a sample medication log for parents and one for teachers as well. The teacher's log is useful because it reflects the judgment of a person who

Sample Medication Logs

For Steven

Start/End	Medication	Dose	+ Effects	− Effects	Comments
9/00-10/00	Ritalin	5-15 mg ams	↑ focus ↑behavior	↓ appetite	Wore off too soon
10/00-11/00	Adderall	10-20 mg ams	↑focus ↑behavior	↓ appetite ↓ sleep	Chewed fingers, looked drugged
11/00-2/01	Metadate ER	20 mg ams	↑focus ↑behavior		Good effects but homework still a problem
2/01–present			↑focus ↑behavior	↓appetite	Minor sleep problems

For Michael

Start/End	Medication	Dose	+ Effects	− Effects	Comments
9/97-10/97	Dexedrine	5 mg, 2X/day		Acted hyper	
10/97-10/99	Ritalin	5 mg- 7.5mg 2-3X/day	↑behavior ↓impulsivity	↓appetite for lunch	Worked for two years
6/99-7/99	Paxil	5-10 mg ams		↓?sleep	Didn't do anything for anger
7/99-7/99	Prozac	10 mg ams		↓ sleep ↑irritable	Didn't do anything for anger
8/99-8/99	Imipramine	10-50 mg ams		↑mild drowsy	Didn't do anything for anger
11/99-5/01	Risperdal	0.25-.5 mg 2X/day	↓intensity & frequency of anger	↑mild sedation ↑↑↑weight	Great effects but gained 20 lbs.
5/01-6/01	Zyprexa	2.5 mg 2X/day		↑sedation	No effect on anger
6/01-present		2X/day	↓frequency of temper tantrums		Tantrums worse, drug not as good as Risperdal

FIGURE 9.1   Sample Medication Logs

sees your child in a significant setting and because the teacher's response is blinded—she doesn't know how much medication the child is receiving and when the dosage has been changed. Admittedly, it's more difficult to get school feedback for high school kids, who usually have a series of teachers instead of just one.

Once your child has been on a steady dose of the medication for a week or two, notes are usually no longer necessary. However, if the med-

NAME OF CHILD_____ NAME OF TEACHER _____

DATE/DAY	DOSAGE (leave blank for parent)		A.M.'s	P.M.'s
			least most	
		IMPULSIVITY	0 1 2 3	0 1 2 3
_____	_____	DISTRACTIBILITY	0 1 2 3	0 1 2 3
		INCOMPLETE TASKS	0 1 2 3	0 1 2 3

comments _____
_____

		IMPULSIVITY	0 1 2 3	0 1 2 3
_____	_____	DISTRACTIBILITY	0 1 2 3	0 1 2 3
		INCOMPLETE TASKS	0 1 2 3	0 1 2 3

comments _____
_____

		IMPULSIVITY	0 1 2 3	0 1 2 3
_____	_____	DISTRACTIBILITY	0 1 2 3	0 1 2 3
		INCOMPLETE TASKS	0 1 2 3	0 1 2 3

comments _____
_____

		IMPULSIVITY	0 1 2 3	0 1 2 3
_____	_____	DISTRACTIBILITY	0 1 2 3	0 1 2 3
		INCOMPLETE TASKS	0 1 2 3	0 1 2 3

comments _____
_____

		IMPULSIVITY	0 1 2 3	0 1 2 3
_____	_____	DISTRACTIBILITY	0 1 2 3	0 1 2 3
		INCOMPLETE TASKS	0 1 2 3	0 1 2 3

comments _____
_____

		IMPULSIVITY	0 1 2 3	0 1 2 3
_____	_____	DISTRACTIBILITY	0 1 2 3	0 1 2 3
		INCOMPLETE TASKS	0 1 2 3	0 1 2 3

comments _____
_____

		IMPULSIVITY	0 1 2 3	0 1 2 3
_____	_____	DISTRACTIBILITY	0 1 2 3	0 1 2 3
		INCOMPLETE TASKS	0 1 2 3	0 1 2 3

comments _____
_____

FIGURE 9.2   Sample Teacher's Log

Blank Medication Log 1

Start/End	Medication	Dose	+ Effects	– Effects	Comments

FIGURE 9.3   Blank Medication Log

ication or dose changes, or if you see persistent alterations in your child's behavior, start keeping track again. This kind of record will be invaluable to any consultant working with you and your child, especially if you change doctors down the road. Previous medical records are often scattered or unavailable to the new physician trying to make decisions.

How Will I Know If My Child Doesn't Need the Drug Anymore?

When a child has a positive response to a drug, and when there are no specific medical indications for more frequent visits, it is good practice for you and your doctor to take stock every six months. A review of changes in the child's behavior and environment is in order: How is the child performing in school? Is there a new teacher? How are parents getting along?

If the child's behavior is satisfactory, you and the doctor could consider a trial period without drugs or on a lower dose of the current medication. Of course, you'll want to solicit the child's opinion on this matter. A surprising number of kids are wary of going drug-free at first. It may take several six-month periods—punctuated by reviews that are consistently full of good news—before they feel comfortable enough to go without the support of medication.

Lots of families, especially those whose kids are on stimulants, accidentally miss dosages here and there. If the child happens to have a bad day on these occasions, the family may be reluctant to undergo a longer drug-free period. However, it takes several days to make a definitive assessment. *One* bad day while off medication doesn't tell me much at all—there are plenty of reasons unrelated to drugs that a child could have a hard time. *Several* bad days in a row are more likely to convince me that the drug should be continued. For a few drugs, especially those like Prozac, it may be necessary to wait a month or longer for the drug to fully clear the system. Until then, you won't know for sure what life off the medication is really like.

Are Brand-Name Drugs Superior to the Generic Versions?

The Food and Drug Administration certifies that a generic drug's active ingredient is the bioequivalent to that of the brand name. Milligram for milligram, they should work the same, and that's been my experience. Rumors and "facts" floating on the Internet may claim that certain brand-name drugs work better than the generic variety, but I have never seen any appreciable difference. That's a good thing—generic drugs are usually less expensive than their brand-name counterparts, and many insurance plans refuse to cover or pay for trade drugs when a generic one is available.

How Can We Remember to
Give Doses at the Right Time?

Taking the right medication at the right time isn't always as easy as it sounds. Studies have shown that compliance with drug regimens goes down dramatically if a pill has to be taken more than twice a day or if more than two drugs are taken simultaneously. And those studies were performed on *adults*. Adding children to the mix makes things even more complicated, as any parent who has tried to implement a nightly ritual of tooth brushing knows.

It's best if the drug can be incorporated into an existing daily routine. In the morning, you might try giving the pill when your child wakes up or as you slip lunch into her backpack for school. Evening doses might be given right after you finish taking out the trash. But one of the factors in a child's behavior problems may be a general lack of family routine and order. If family life is especially erratic, the child might be given a pill by a member of the school staff when she arrives in the morning. When all the adults in the household work and afternoon dosing is required, you will need to make arrangements with a trusted caregiver or, again, with school personnel.

Finally, teens who take doses of a stimulant drug during the day should never be given extra pills to take to school. There is simply too much pressure on even the most responsible of children to sell or trade the medication. When a doctor explains this rule in a straightforward manner, the teen will usually accept it.

Will the Drug Ever Stop Working?

True physical tolerance—meaning that more and more of a drug is needed to achieve the same effects—occurs only with the benzodiazepines like Valium and Xanax. However, a common development is that a psychoactive drug "works" for weeks, months, or years—and then the child experiences a recurrence of the original problem or a new difficulty altogether. In a few circumstances, the dosage may need to be increased if the child has grown or gained weight. But dosages of most psychoactive drugs are not determined by body mass.

In one study, children diagnosed with ADHD were asked to check groups of rapidly appearing letters or numbers for patterns and errors. When they were given stimulants and asked to take the test a second time, they all showed improvement. The kids were followed for several years. Some of them—now mostly young teenagers—began having problems again. The entire group returned to the laboratory for the same kind of test. To the doctors' surprise, *all* of the children—the ones who were doing well and the ones with problems—showed the same level of performance improvement when on the stimulant.

My own conclusion is that the stimulants had not stopped working for the problematic group. Rather, these kids simply had more or new problems. They may have been disposed toward more difficulties, or perhaps their environment had changed for the worse. Medications can affect the neurosynaptic milieu only to a degree, and chemical changes caused by a difficult environment may overwhelm whatever benefits a drug may offer.

If a child exhibits new or recurring problems after a period of success with a drug, the child's total situation should be reviewed once again. Has the family undergone major changes since the original prescription? Are assignments at school getting tougher, or are there entirely new social pressures? If environmental changes do not help or are not possible, the doctor might switch to a different drug or try an increased dose of the original. One popular strategy is to add a new drug to the existing regimen. But given the increased risk of side effects and other complications of polypharmacy (the use of multiple drugs), I am reluctant to pile up medications.

Do I Have to Change My Child's Diet?

The answer is no, unless your child is one of the very few kids taking monoamine oxidase inhibitors. These drugs are used so rarely in children that I do not list them in this book. They call for strict dietary restrictions, and even items like cheddar cheese are off the menu if the child is to avoid serious complications.

What About Over-the-Counter Medications?

The Food and Drug Administration's safety standards virtually assure that over-the-counter medications will not interact with prescription drugs. However, some cold medications contain antihistamines, which can intensify sleepiness in kids who are already taking sedating drugs. And some of the newer seasonal allergy medicines may interact with the SSRIs, theoretically creating a risk for a heart arrhythmia, which can be serious. It's a good idea to check with your doctor about both of these possible combinations. In general, over-the-counter drugs are not an issue, but if you're at all uncertain, check with your doctor or pharmacist.

Should I Consult the *Physician's Desk Reference* or the Internet for More Information About Psychiatric Drugs?

The *Physician's Desk Reference* (PDR), a compendium of prescription drugs and their side effects, is essentially a legal document required by the FDA. At the other end of the reference spectrum is the freewheeling and unregulated Internet. Both can be useful, but you need to understand their peculiar limitations.

The PDR lists every possible side effect a drug might have, often leaving the reader with little perspective on the actual degree of risk. Aspirin, for example, is listed in the PDR in combination with other drugs; when you look it up, you see that it entails a risk of stroke. But that risk is so rare that millions of people take aspirin every day. Anyone who reads the PDR and its warnings could not be blamed for never agreeing to take *any* drug again. But some parents like having it around. They know that if their child experiences an ailment, they can check the PDR to see if it is possibly drug-related.

The Internet is supposedly the great democratizer of information, but the online world continues to perpetuate old and new urban legends—and that is as true for drugs as for reports of criminal conspiracies. If you like using the Internet, by all means keep exploring. But you need to weigh the information you find based on the reliability of the source, not on whether it appears to make sense (inaccurate information is often compelling). Web sites maintained by the U.S. government, as well as respected professional medical organizations and self-help groups, are usually trustworthy; just watch out for a strong tendency to promote biochemical theories of personality and drug solutions over all else. If your child has been diagnosed with ADHD, you may want to visit the PBS *Frontline* Web site at www.pbs.org/wgbh/pages/frontline. Its "Medicating Kids" page provides a wide spectrum of responsible views of ADHD and medications.

Can I Use Alternative Medicine Instead of a Pill?

Most herbs, special diets, and other forms of alternative medicine have simply not been studied sufficiently for me to give you a clear yes or no as to their effectiveness and safety.

Some parents ask about sugar and food additives. The Feingold diet, which eliminates refined sugars, food additives and colorings, and salicylates (chemicals that give foods like oranges and tomatoes their tang), purports to decrease hyperactivity and has a dedicated following. But good studies show that refined sugars and salicylates do not cause or exacerbate children's behavior problems. However, one well-conducted study demonstrated that huge amounts of food coloring, specifically red dye number two, increases irritability in children five years old and younger. I think it's reasonable to limit processed foods—junk food and convenience items—and buy more organic ingredients or cook more meals from scratch. But given the limited amount of evidence for dietary interventions, I'd still rather have Mom confronting Johnny over putting away his toys instead of battling him over eating a cupcake.

Biofeedback and neurofeedback, in which a person learns to control involuntary physiological responses, have been proven useful for stress-related conditions in adults. On the surface, they appear to make sense for psychological conditions that obviously have some neurophysiological components, like ADHD or anxiety. But these treatments take a lot of time and are often expensive, and as yet there are no large, controlled studies that convincingly demonstrate their effectiveness for behavioral problems in children.

I would be wary of various herbs and supplements, which tend to follow a cycle of momentary popularity before fading from public awareness. Because they are not considered drugs by the FDA, they are not held to the same stringent standards for safety and production. The manufacturers are permitted to make vague but fervent proclamations about their effectiveness, even in the absence of proof. Nor are systematic investigations likely to occur anytime soon, since manufacturers prefer to avoid deep scrutiny of loose claims like "improves attention and focus."

St. John's wort for depression, kava kava for anxiety, and valerian root for sleep are all at a peak of profitability right now, and they may indeed have some positive effects. But none of them has been studied well in children. They can also interact with other drugs and cause worrisome side effects. It's possible that melatonin, a hormone that rode a crest of public enthusiasm a few years back, can help children fall asleep; unlike the other products listed here, it appears to be pretty safe. But *always* talk with a doctor before giving an herb or a supplement to a child.

About half of all Americans have tried alternative medicine. I suspect that rates are even higher for families frustrated or frightened by the heavy use of psychiatric drugs in response to children's behavioral or emotional problems. With time and study, some of these alternative treatments may prove to be useful. But rarely are there simple answers to these kinds of problems. Finding an honest and caring professional who will take time with your family will go a long way toward helping you and your child cope—without resorting to untried and unproven interventions.

PART TWO

Specific Help for
Specific Problems

10

Intense, Distractible, Energetic, Angry: Kids Who Act Out

Nine-year-old Stephen still gets out of his seat at school and shouts out of turn. He plays with the pencils in his desk instead of getting down to work. "He's distracted by molecules of *air*," his father tells me with a groan. Stephen listens to the teacher when she disciplines him, but at home he ignores or rages against his parents, especially his mother. During time-outs, he trashes his room and destroys valued toys in his anger. He teases his younger sister constantly. Recently he was caught stealing a pocket knife from a hardware store.

Much has already been said in this book about kids like Stephen. Problems similar to his—trouble in the classroom, battling limits, hitting and biting, even stealing—send worried parents into my office every day. The standard professional approach to these children is to locate their problems within the framework of increasingly popular diagnoses, most often ADHD or ODD but also conduct and bipolar disorders. Let's take a look at each diagnosis.

Let the Diagnosis Fit the Drug?

So is Stephen ADHD or oppositional defiant disorder (ODD)? Is he showing early signs of a conduct or bipolar disorder? Does he have one condition or perhaps two or three?

Well, the ADHD diagnosis is applied mostly to kids exhibiting hyperactivity, impulsivity, and lack of focus. So far, Stephen appears inattentive and at times impulsive. He is not particularly hyper.

Might he have ODD, then? Oppositional defiant disorder is a slightly different category used for children who battle their parents over normal, daily limits. A typical child who "has" ODD will fight any command or activity that doesn't promise instantaneous fun. Every limit transaction becomes a potential drama with these kids. More serious ODD may be diagnosed when parents wait on pins and needles every time they issue a limit, bracing themselves for an explosion. Kids—especially those seven and older—who use physical violence and aggression, get into fights repeatedly on the playground, hit a teacher, or lose control in the principal's office may also receive a "serious ODD" diagnosis (as may younger kids who do things like "accidentally" hurling a toy at a sister's eye). From what little we know of Stephen, he might fit the ODD profile. But he doesn't defy authority figures other than his parents on a regular basis.

The symptoms of ADHD or ODD can be very similar; although there is a more negative spin on the testing behaviors of ODD, children in both categories have trouble performing if there isn't an immediate reward. Some people try to delineate between the two by claiming that whereas ADHD children can't control themselves, ODD children simply won't. But attempts to tease out a clear difference in motivation belies the complexity of human behavior. Another way a professional might try to account for the indistinct quality of these and other categories is to diagnose Stephen with "co-morbid" ADHD and ODD—meaning that he has both.

If, as a teenager, Stephen hurts someone who files charges with the police, he may be diagnosed with conduct disorder. A major step up from ODD, conduct disorder is characterized by stealing, substance abuse, and other acts of delinquency. That trouble with the law has become, in essence, a psychiatric condition poses a philosophical conundrum. If conduct disorder is a viable diagnosis, is there anyone in prison who doesn't have it? (Interestingly, the law does not let a person free simply for "having" a psychiatric disorder. An insanity defense supposedly requires that the person be unable to tell the difference between right and wrong—a limitation that is not automatically included in the diagnoses of ODD, conduct disorder, or even antisocial personality disorder, the ultimate sociopathic diagnosis. However, those who can afford the legal machinery are often able to exploit the psychiatric DSM to receive mitigated sentences.)

Bipolar disorder is the final car on this train of diagnoses, and it is the most controversial. Until the mid-1990s, most child psychiatrists believed this diagnosis—which replaced manic depression in the DSM—to be rare in children. Symptoms included mania, euphoria, or grandiosity, along with an inability to distinguish fantasy from reality. Characteristic periods of extreme highs or lows would last for months or weeks. But in 1996, Joseph Biederman, chief of the Harvard Pediatric Psychopharmacology Clinic, published a paper claiming that 23 percent of their ADHD children also had bipolar disorder. The Harvard group had always found higher rates of co-morbidity in their ADHD patients, and admittedly its practice attracts kids whose problems are extreme. But this rate of bipolar disease in children astonished the world of academic child psychiatry.

Biederman further claimed that these bipolar kids were marked by a different set of symptoms from those found in adults. Unless they were enraged, they knew the difference between fantasy and reality. They "cycled" through moods several times over the course of a single day—an observation that gave pause to most people familiar with the habits of children and teens. Thanks in part to these new criteria, the once harmless and common description of a child or teen as "moody" or "having mood swings" has become potentially loaded with implications of pathology. The kids in Biederman's group didn't have to exhibit the classic signs of mania (euphoria, grandiosity, and hyperenergy) at all. They were mostly angry and irritable, unhappy, and difficult to control.

Biederman felt that children diagnosed as bipolar could be saved from a lifetime of antisocial behavior and substance abuse through aggressive treatment with medication. According to the Harvard group, the presumed hereditary and biochemical nature of bipolar disorder justified the use of much more serious medications: lithium, Depakote, Neurontin—all drugs with far more serious short- and long-term side effects than Ritalin.

The response from other academic researchers was mixed. Debate continues in the professional journals over the definition and frequency of bipolar disorder in children. One psychiatrist, echoing some of my own worries, commented cynically that "Ritalin is for irritable and irritating children while lithium is for *very* irritable and *very* irritating children."

The practical effect, though, of the announcement of this new interpretation of pediatric bipolar disorder is the growing use of serious medications for kids. Several hundred thousand children take heavy-duty "mood-stabilizing drugs" for purported bipolar disorder with scant evidence of even short-term effectiveness and safety. Most are teens, but some are children as young as three. The bipolar diagnosis implies a serious mental illness, a lifelong disorder requiring treatment (although I take issue with this stance; I think it is incorrectly based on older studies of manic-depressives, whose diagnoses required a more restrictive set of symptoms). Labeling kids and teens with a lifelong disorder (implying lifelong pharmaceutical treatment) deeply concerns me. What if some of these admittedly troubled children are simply struggling mightily through one phase of their lives?

In psychiatry, as in the rest of medicine, diagnosis supposedly determines treatment. But when it comes to kids' behavior problems, there's a disturbing amount of crossover among the categories—much like the old "unscientific" days of the Freudian diagnoses.

With so much blurring among the disorders, the response to drugs is the factor that often drives diagnosis. If Stephen doesn't improve sufficiently on one medication (say, Ritalin for ADHD), another disorder may be invoked to justify adding another drug to his program. I have seen children classified with three separate disorders and taking three or four separate medications simultaneously—a desperate clustering of labels and drugs triggered mainly by the failure of any single drug to help. This tactic is disparagingly known as "diagnosis through pharmacological dissection." But it is the reality of frontline pediatric psychiatry.

Acting Out: An Alternative "Diagnosis"

Instead of trying to parse Stephen's symptoms into smudged diagnostic categories, I prefer to think of them as belonging to the broad group of behaviors called *acting out,* which describes a pattern of response to stress. When acting-out children feel under the gun, they want to take over the situation or throw a punch. They can often be classified as having difficult temperaments—persistent, impulsive, intense, and energetic from birth. At the risk of gross stereotyping, boys tend to act out, while girls tend to act in (they try to satisfy and please when stressed). But there is no rule that an individual girl can't stab another child with a pencil or that a boy won't pursue straight A's as a means of coping.

Acting out is a large category to be sure, but ultimately it's more pragmatic and honest than pretending there are clean distinctions between kids who hit (who are labeled with serious ODD) and kids who break the law by hitting (who are labeled with conduct disorder). Nor have I found many differences among the approaches that help kids who "have" ADHD versus those who meet the criteria for a different set of acting-out symptoms.

Is It Depression?

Common folk psychology sees depression as anger at others turned inward. Although many of the children I see are very unhappy with themselves and their lives, I still hesitate to label them as "depressed." Depression in children rarely presents as the adult form—severe withdrawal, loss of energy, lack of appetite, weight loss, the inability or desire to have pleasure. Most of the "depressed" children I meet are actually agitated and impulsive. They are less able to delay gratification, which they still vigorously pursue.

Sounds a lot like an acting-out child, right? Sometimes, as these kids receive more and more negative feedback about themselves, they become more and more unhappy. If you can speak to them when they're calm and not feeling at risk of judgment, they tell you how bad they feel about themselves—that they are bad or dumb, or that their families would be better off without them. But you would never guess it from their regular behaviors.

I'm not suggesting that we add depression to the list of labels applied to kids who act out. Too many children are diagnosed as "depressed" mainly to justify adding second or third medications when stimulants alone are not working. In reality, the sad undercurrent that can run beneath the behavior of these active, sometimes lively, children speaks to the extent to which personality defies tidy categories and set responses. The problems of these kids call out for help, but not necessarily through pharmaceutical means. Changing the child's environment and behavior can often lead to more positive patterns of success.

Options for Acting-Out Problems

Behavioral Interventions

I don't blame parents for their kids' acting-out problems. Children who act out are often temperamentally challenging, and they are not easy children to raise. They require a degree of consistency and an immediacy of response that is not exactly a snap to deliver—and is much harder to accomplish in an era of demanding schedules, long commutes, and pressure-cooker lives, when parents are less supported and more likely to question their child-rearing abilities than in the past.

Parents are further handicapped by what I call politically correct parenting advice, vestigial notions from the Freudian era brought to American homes by Benjamin Spock and those who follow in his footsteps. Spock's advice to be more flexible, use reasoning, and induce guilt as primary methods of discipline appeared a necessary corrective to American parenting style in the first half of the twentieth century, which now seems so constricted and cold. But as a sole guide to raising children today, the politically correct approach cripples all but the most self-confident parents from doing what's necessary for our children of today, the ones who have no trouble at all emoting but won't listen to adults. I'm not calling for a return to the bad old days. I *am* asking parents to set limits with a little less of the guilt and doubt that now seems so rampant in American parenting culture.

Children who act out—whether they "have" ADHD, ODD, conduct disorder, bipolar disorder, or whatever other diagnoses come down the pike—respond positively to strategies that I describe in this book. To review: Parents should provide a loving environment with limits that are enforced in a steady, consistent fashion. Since acting-out children tend to be caught up in their impulses, cajoling and threats of delayed consequences do not work well with them. Black-and-white choices ("Stephen, stop teasing your sister or I'm sending you to time-out"), followed up by quick action, work best. Immediate rewards can motivate the good behavior that is a struggle for the intense, persistent, and difficult child. Externalizing the problem can empower families to set and follow limits without engaging in lots of blaming and self-recrimination. Parents who are too busy, overwhelmed, or stressed by marital conflict to provide a steady environment for these kids may need to work on their own problems before they can help their children.

Since acting-out behaviors often go hand in hand with learning problems, kids should be screened for learning disabilities. Parents should make a concerted attempt at finding a classroom that is tailored to their child's learning and behavioral needs. A teacher who provides the child with immediate feedback and a system of rewards and punishments can be a godsend.

EXTREME KIDS, EXTREME INTERVENTIONS

Some kids exhibit acting-out behavior that is dangerous to themselves or others. Fourteen-year-old Sarah is an example. Her parents were divorced when she was two, and until recently she had been living with her mother, Terry. But Terry drew the line at Sarah's violence. It's not unusual for Sarah to throw things at her in anger. Terry has also been worried about her daughter's promiscuity—she looks eighteen and has admitted to giving oral sex to older boys in the park after school. When Sarah wanted to stay out with some high school seniors until one in the morning, she and Terry ended up grappling on the floor until Sarah's brother broke them up. Later that month, Sarah attacked a girl who called her a slut.

In most cases, a coordinated, consistent approach to discipline, like the one outlined in Chapter 4, will help even very aggressive children. Children who've experienced divorce or some other traumatic event can also benefit from time with an understanding professional.

But when consistent discipline doesn't work or cannot be delivered in the child's current environment, parents need to consider changing that environment. They may be faced with agonizing choices, like sending the child to relatives, a special (and expensive) boarding school, or even a county-sponsored group home that is better equipped to provide consistent support. I have seen some parents choose to let their delinquent child go to a juvenile detention center, and I have supported their decision, albeit with sadness. Sometimes it's the only way to keep children from hurting themselves or other people.

As it turned out, neither parent was able to provide Sarah the kind of consistency she needed (very few parents could have). After the school incident, Sarah entered an anger-management program and moved in with her father, Arnold. But there was literally no place in his house for Sarah. She slept on his living room sofa for a few weeks before running away; her parents were frantic until she came home three days later.

I have been seeing Sarah once a week to offer support, but she may not be willing to take advantage of outside help until she hits rock bottom. Her parents are working with me too, as they try to get on the same page with their rules and standards. Given their temperamental differences—Terry is sensitive and Arnold is rather inflexible—it's a challenge.

Sarah's behavior right now puts herself and others in jeopardy. Placing her with another family, perhaps a trusted friend or relative, was one option, but no one wanted to take Sarah after the running-away fiasco. We talked about sending her to an Outward Bound course for a couple of weeks, but neither Terry nor Arnold has the funds. Until we can find a more controlled environment for Sarah than her father's house, I'm willing to try medications. On a superficial level, Sarah is willing to admit she has some problems and says that she will take medication. But I'm worried: Her willpower vanishes when she is enraged. Will she really take medication on a consistent basis?

Sarah had been given two different stimulant medications when she was younger; the drugs had helped, but her arguments and flashes of anger continued. After a few years without taking prescription drugs at all, she has begun Wellbutrin, which may be useful for kids with a combination of acting-out behaviors and depressive symptoms. It's also a good option for teens who might be tempted to abuse stimulants. (Sarah definitely falls into that category.) It's too early to tell if the drug is having much effect. Of course, I would far prefer finding her a safe and secure environment in which to work things out.

I suspect that many of the children who are carrying a bipolar diagnosis and receiving heavy medications are kids like Sarah, the ones who have no place to go. When a solution for violent and dangerous behavior can not be found privately, public institutions—like the juvenile justice system—may step in. I hope Sarah and her family will find some other resolution of her most immediate problems, even if drugs are part of the solution.

INTERVENING WITH TODDLERS

Little Helene was almost three, but she already had a pistol of a personality. She threw multiple fits at home every day, and she had just been asked to leave her parent-run preschool because of her regular tantrums. Helene's parents, Carla and Earl, who adopted their daughter at birth, were stumped.

In my office, Helene at first played rather nicely with her parents and the toys. But as the session progressed, she became freer and freer in her play. At one point, I was talking to her parents when a Tinker Toy whizzed past my ear.

"Helene, you come here this minute," Carla said. Helene, looking both embarrassed and defiant, didn't budge. "I'm counting," Carla told her. "That's one . . . two . . . If I get to three you'll lose your cookies tonight."

Helene took a tentative step toward her mother. Hey, I said to myself, Carla's doing well.

"Why did you throw the toy at the doctor?" Carla asked Helene.

Uh-oh, I thought. One step backward for Carla. "Why" questions rarely help in these situations. Helene refused to answer, lost her cookies for the evening, and then threw a tantrum in my office.

Afterward, I talked with the parents alone. Helene wasn't a bad girl; she was an intense, persistent, and sensitive child who was seeking demonstrations of steadiness from her parents. I thought the parents, especially Carla, were already showing a lot of skill and thought in raising Helene. They just needed some "fine-tuning"—support to diminish their ambivalence. We went over the one, two, three time-out process, along with the twin needs for immediacy and action. I told them to drop the questioning stuff and expectations of apology. It was simply too hard for little Helene, whose brain was showing early signs of "vapor lock"—that confused state of mind found in explosive children. Both Carla and Earl felt that my suggestions made sense, and they agreed to try them out at home.

After about two weeks, Carla and Earl came back, wearing broad smiles of pride and pleasure. They reported that once they became consistent with the one-two-three time-out process (and Earl especially got involved in the action), Helene was a "changed person." She listened to them, threw very few tantrums, and was actually more affectionate than ever. When I next saw the whole family, I caught myself thinking: It's as if Helene had taken a drug. She was much calmer and seemed happier as all four of us enjoyed a charades game for kids. I saw a few signs of testing behavior, but Carla and Earl were on the ball, intervening early and intimating that Helene might have to go to time-out in the doctor's office, and reminding her of the trip to McDonald's after our meeting if she kept her temper in check.

This kind of rapid turnaround when parents agree on limits and act consistently used to surprise me. Over the years, I've learned that it's not unusual, especially in toddlers. It is deeply distressing for parents when a younger child exhibits behavior problems like Helene's—even more so when the result is banishment from a preschool or kindergarten. But toddlers are highly responsive to alterations in parenting practice, and changes at home often provide them with the extra steadiness they crave.

Pharmaceutical Interventions

The majority of families I see have significant success in helping acting-out children at home and at school without the initial use of a medication. Yet some parents feel that no matter what they try, their children continue to struggle. Even when there are positive changes at home, there may be ongoing trouble in class. The decision to use medication with a child who has acting-out problems is ultimately a personal choice between parents, child, and doctor; frequently, the deciding factors are continuing problems at school and a sense that the child's self-esteem is declining or at risk. Although the evidence is mixed that children whose performance and behavior improve with medication feel better about themselves, many parents in these situations are ready for their children to experience the clear short-term benefits of drugs.

With their relative safety and short-term effectiveness proven over sixty years of use, stimulant medications like Ritalin and Adderall are the overwhelming first choice of medicines for acting-out problems. I write prescriptions for these drugs regularly—although I strongly believe and advocate that parents and schools continue behavioral and learning interventions, even when a medication appears to be working.

The vast majority of children—estimates range from 60 to 90 percent—with ADHD-type symptoms improve with just a stimulant. A stimulant drug is based on either methylphenidate or amphetamine, and if a child does not improve with one, the other should be tried before giving up. Parents should be sure that the doctor methodically increases the dosage every three to four days, to the point where either the behavior is clearly improved or unpleasant side effects persist. Too frequently, parents who have tried stimulants before, tell me that their child does not respond to them. But then I learn that because of their ambivalence about using the drug or because they lacked proper information from a doctor, the family gave up after the child tried no more than the lowest possible dosage.

Children who make a thorough trial of stimulants but are not helped at all are often very angry, very anxious, or very sad. Invariably, their home and school environments are heavily problematic. The decision to move on from the stimulant class to other medications (often they are prescribed in addition to a stimulant) is a much more complicated one for parents, loaded with difficult questions about efficacy and side effects.

Second-line medications for acting-out symptoms include clonidine and Tenex, whose sedating factor makes them attractive for symptoms that occur later in the day. Tricyclics may still be used when depression is thought to be a part of the child's problem. All of these medications are controversial; there is increasing skepticism about their overall effectiveness and concern over side effects that can, in extremely rare circumstances, include death. Two other drugs, Wellbutrin and Effexor, are being used as second-choice medications more and more often, especially for the ADHD symptom of impulsivity, but again, little is known about their effects, good and bad, on children.

Another possible and increasingly well-traveled medication route for acting-out problems includes adding Prozac or one of the ever growing class of SSRI medications to a stimulant drug. They have not proven themselves particularly useful for kids with these kinds of problems, but they may be employed if a doctor suspects that depression or undue sensitivity is an element of the child's difficulties—or simply if her behavior continues to be a serious issue and the doctor is stumped.

The next group of drugs for acting out are the anticonvulsants, antipsychotics (novel and traditional), and lithium—the "big guns" like Depakote or Risperdal with side effects to match. They have traditionally been used only in the most severe cases, but I am seeing more and more children who take them in response to the increasingly popular but fuzzy bipolar diagnosis. The antipsychotics, because of their sedating qualities as well as risks of weight gain and a permanent, involuntary movement disorder, should be employed only as a last resort in the increasingly risky act of balancing symptom reduction against side effects. Parents who are considering them are usually facing additional hard questions about the child's environment, including placement in a special class or residential program. There may be issues at home regarding serious marital problems or the safety of the child. When this group of drugs is being considered, all choices feel lousy. The decisionmakers—generally parents and doctors—need to be closely in tune with one another.

11

Shy, Sensitive, Fearful: Kids Who Act In

Whenever she was out in public, seven-year-old Samantha clung to her mother's leg like a frightened mouse. The year before, when Sam was in first grade, it could take half an hour to pry her loose and usher her into class. According to her current teacher, Sam was quiet and unsmiling, afraid to raise her hand if she wasn't 100 percent certain she knew the answer to a question.

But at home, Sam dominated the household. Her tantrums were legendary; despite her mother's attempts at consolation, they could go on for hours. Nor did anyone know what would set Sam off next. She screamed when her mother brushed her hair. She was a finicky eater, upset by details that other children wouldn't even notice—for instance, her corn being heated in the microwave instead of on the stovetop. She insisted on wearing the same pair of pants to school every day, which meant that her mother had to wash and dry them each night. She couldn't sleep after sunrise because the sound of birds chirping bothered her.

"Sam is miserable and I don't know what to do," said Kathleen, Sam's mother, who looked pretty miserable herself. Two months earlier, Sam had been playing in the park when she was startled—but not stung—by a bee. Since then, Sam had developed a growing fear of all insects. During a recent summer heat wave, when Kathleen proposed a visit to the local water theme park, Sam screamed and yelled at the mere suggestion. Arthur, Sam's little brother, couldn't understand why he was being denied his fun. Lately, Sam had been reluctant to go outside at all, even on a nice day.

Even before the bee incident, Kathleen had felt the need for outside help and took Sam to a developmental pediatrician. He thought that Sam was anxious and prescribed Prozac. When that didn't help, he tried Paxil, a similar drug. Sam then took Ritalin, Zoloft, Dexedrine, clonidine, Klonopin, and imipramine—sometimes individually, sometimes in combination with one another—over the next nine months.

As Sam marched through this psychotropic drug parade, Kathleen, a part-time social worker, grew increasingly skeptical. She felt that the drugs, far from helping, created additional sleep and behavior problems for her daughter. When she came to me, she was seeking another opinion and was ready to try some nonpharmaceutical approaches to help Sam.

Acting-In Problems

I was a bit horrified (and, in a stunned fashion, even impressed) by the number of drugs this little girl had taken. I imagined the diagnoses the doctor might have applied to Sam to justify the various drugs he had given her: generalized anxiety disorder, school phobia, panic disorder, attention deficit/hyperactivity disorder, obsessive-compulsive disorder, dysthymia (feeling blue), depression, or, since Sam's parents had divorced a few years ago, posttraumatic stress disorder.

From a practical point of view, these diagnoses are about as helpful as the medieval theological debate over how many angels can dance on the head of a pin. The large amount of crossover and blending among the categories renders them nearly useless for the meaningful ends of diagnosis—to determine what is going on with the child, what to do about the problem, and what the future portends. Instead of trying to make nice divisions among blurred categories and affixing two or three or four indistinct labels to a child, it's more helpful to think of the symptoms as belonging to a much broader group—internalizing or acting-in problems.

Kids who act out respond to stress by trying to take over or hit someone—the old "fight-or-flight" response described by ethnopsychologists of the early twentieth century. But other kids respond to stress by turning their feelings inward; we say they "act in." They withdraw; they analyze and worry; they try to please; they draw their hurt and anger inside themselves.

Although gender differences are by no means universal, boys who are under stress tend to act out, whereas girls will often act in. These tendencies are likely both biological (in the "wiring") and culturally determined. Videotaped studies of parents playing with their babies show that both boys and girls are bounced up and down on their parents' knees. The boys usually gurgle with delight and excitement, which encourages the parents to increase the activity and prolong it. The girls generally show a bit more hesitation and discomfort—and the parents react by bouncing with less vigor and for shorter periods of time. The different responses boy and girl babies have to rougher play begins a feedback loop between the child and parents, one that reinforces the pattern of more activity for the boys and less for the girls.

Different patterns of coping with stress—whether a child tends to act in or act out—probably evolve in a similar way for young children. Infant temperament experts have documented qualities like regularity of sleeping and eating, ability to handle change, and consolability in the first hours and days of life. Researchers like T. Berry Brazelton and Jerome Kagan have demonstrated that some children can be described as highly sensitive from birth. They might also have a low tolerance for frustration and a tendency to withdraw and seek succor in

response to stress. Like acting-out children, these kids are more vulnerable to problems later in life and more difficult to parent. However, the experts also emphasize that temperament is not destiny; how
parents participate in that feedback loop of behavior and response
may be just as important. Parents who are also sensitive and prone to
worry may unintentionally reinforce the child's problematic behavior;
they are more likely to scoop their sensitive child into their arms at
the slightest sign of distress, unwittingly reinforcing the child's uncer-
tainty and desire for rescue. But an appreciation of the child's unique
personality, combined with firm but kind insistence on participation
in the world, can encourage the child toward greater resilience.

You might think that sensitive kids would be shy around the clock,
but Sam, who was quiet at school and demanding with her family, fit
a familiar pattern. Of the acting-in cases in my office, a very small
minority can be characterized by inhibited behavior at home. Even
sensitive teenagers, who want to be left alone in their rooms, will
often make many demands of their parents.

As I've noted before, it's not always easy to draw a clear line between acting-in and acting-out behavior. Children who are agitated
and impulsive may also be quite sad. And kids who feel incompetent
and worried may respond by withdrawing in public while at the same
time becoming more tyrannical at home. Nearly all sensitive kids
warm up to their environment and are comfortable enough on their
own turf to demand—aggressively—the kind of rescuing behavior
they crave (as in "Don't make me try this new toy" or "Don't make me
go to *Indian Princesses* tonight").

New situations usually lead to the typical inhibition and worry.
With time, children often adjust to school or camp or Mom's new
boyfriend and improve. But if the environment is inhospitable or un-
sympathetic, or if the child's behavior somehow starts a vicious cir-
cle—say, if a withdrawn child is teased by others, leading to more
withdrawal and more teasing—the symptoms may worsen.

When this cycle of inhibition, withdrawal, rescue, and loss of competency persists into the teenage years, it becomes much more difficult for parents and doctors to do something about it. Acting-in teens must face their problems largely on their own, often by hitting the wall—becoming depressed. Hitting the wall might take the form of a prolonged school-avoidance episode or complete social withdrawal from friends and the outside world. Teens, understandably, feel deeply sad at these circumstances; they may feel paralyzed and incapable of changing them. And then there's the group of teens, who, much like some adults, respond to new stresses by becoming sad and depressed. The loss of a boyfriend or girlfriend, alienation and loneliness, their parents' divorce, a continually abusive situation at home, or persistent failure at school can trigger a more adult-like bout of depression in some teens.

Options for Kids Who Act In

Behavioral Interventions

Samantha's future, based on Kathleen's descriptions, seemed guarded at best. She certainly was on her way to appearing odder and odder, and the increasing constrictions to her daily activity would eventually leave her feeling incompetent compared with other children her age. She seemed to be caught in an endless cycle of fear, panic, tantrums, and sadness. And Kathleen, who loved Sam dearly, felt helpless to come to her daughter's aid.

When the time came for the family visit, Kathleen limped into the office as if there were a large tumor attached to her left leg. Sam wasn't budging. Kathleen told me that she and Kathleen's stepfather, Mike, practically had to pull her into the car to get to the appointment. So I expected Sam and I wouldn't have much of a conversation. But I was wrong: Sam could talk. She was articulate and forthright about her fears and even related her bee story with dramatic relish. Later, the family played together and drew a picture as a group. Both parents connected well to the children, and they obviously enjoyed one another's company.

Toward the end of the visit, I asked the family why they thought Sam had her problem. All fell silent. Kathleen finally ventured that the previous doctor thought Sam suffered from a chemical imbalance. Arthur, the little brother, didn't understand, so Kathleen's mother tried to explain. When she was done, Arthur proclaimed, "Oh, I knew that already. Her brain is broken."

The family had come to believe that Sam couldn't help herself—how could she, with that broken brain? Kathleen felt so sorry for her anxious little girl that she stopped enforcing the house rules, feeling that Sam suffered enough without the additional pain of parental limits. But this tactic had not helped. Nor had patient attempts to reassure and soothe Sam or to let her give constant voice to her fears. Mike tried to use logic to cut through Sam's obsession. "What's the real chance of being stung?" he asked her. "Have you ever been stung before?" But Sam— who was certainly capable of answering his questions intelligently— would shrug and murmur, "I don't know." She sensed that she was being cornered into an admission she wasn't ready to make.

When I spoke to Kathleen and Mike later, we agreed that reasoning and reassurance had fallen flat. I tried to redirect the parents' sympathy and efforts at helping their poor, stuck child in this way: "Sam feels controlled and bossed around by her thoughts. She cannot free herself, so you'll have to help her. Reasoning doesn't work because the fears are not the outcome of a rational process. Trying to help her think through her problems is just frustrating everyone. No, the way to help Sam is first to free *yourselves* from the tyranny of her fears. *You* need to refuse to be bossed around by her obsessions."

Mike and Kathleen could start by setting limits. When a three-year-old (or five-year-old or even nine-year-old) child refuses to come into my office or tries to crawl under her mother's sweater, the parents can say (in an authoritative but kind voice), "You're old enough to sit next to me without trying to reenter my womb. If you can't sit here nicely, you'll have to sit by yourself." When an acting-in teenager who's been avoiding school won't speak during the family session, the parent could say, sympathetically, "I can't help you if you don't try to participate here. We may just have to sit in silence. But you'll be dealing with the school tomorrow by yourself when you don't show up for class." In both cases, the demand is delivered clearly but with appreciation for the child's temperament, as if to say: "We know it's harder for you to do these things, but we believe you *can* do them, and we will insist on it." Just as with acting-out kids, appropriate limits give shy kids a sense of security and comfort. They also break that feedback loop of children's behavior and parental responses that encourage it.

Kathleen and I initially worked out limits for Sam; at the same time, we externalized her problem as Timmy's parents had done with their son. In her one-on-one meeting with me, Sam decided to name her fears (in perhaps not the most original of inspirations) "Mr. Fear." I reminded her that Mr. Fear was not a real person but represented the fears and emotions that wouldn't let her act the way she wanted to. We drew up an anxiety thermometer and agreed that Sam could tackle some of her lower-grade worries, like walking to the car from the house. (Her "hottest" fear was visiting the park where the bee had grazed her.) She would need courage to face her enemy, but she would have help from her parents, especially her mother.

"Your mom is going to stand up to Mr. Fear too," I told Sam. Katherine could tell Sam that it was okay to be upset, but when she felt that way she was better off in her room. Katherine could then engage in some enticing activity like cooking, which Sam enjoyed, that would shift the focus away from the bees. Sad, anxious children like Sam benefit from talk and support, but there is a limit to that benefit. Continued talk without any change in behavior tends to contribute to the problem. (When kids or teens have experienced acute or ongoing trauma, there is a larger role for the doctor or therapist who spends supportive one-on-one time with the child. And of course, the larger environment *must* be considered and addressed when there is marital or postdivorce strife, abuse, neglect, or serious teasing and bullying.)

Reward systems, like limits, are not limited to use with hyper, impulsive kids; they can also have a role in encouraging more activity and participation from sensitive children. We worked out a plan in which Katherine would reward Sam with a quarter for just going out to the car and back without fussing, even when it wasn't necessary to go anywhere. Mike would do the same. But if Sam didn't cooperate when the family needed to go out, she wouldn't earn her quarter— *and* she'd be carried by her parents to the car without any discussion. We explained it all to Sam. Even with the aversive element included, she liked the plan and thought she could do it.

Katherine, Mike, and Samantha returned in a week, proud that Sam had earned three dollars in quarters. And something else had happened. Katherine sounded clearer and stronger than she had on the previous appointments. While Samantha was still frightened of the bees, Katherine spent much less time talking and fretting about the problem herself. She even battled Samantha successfully over the morning hair-brushing traumas. "I told her that if she let me brush her hair before school without complaining, she could watch some TV before we left for school. But if she complained, I'd stop brushing and Sam would have to go to school without her hair looking the way she likes it. I meant it too. I just got tired of catering to Mr. Fear."

Katherine, it appeared, decided on her own to broaden the front against Mr. Fear to include other behaviors that had plagued Samantha, with the reinstitution of limits, rules, and specific rewards as her tools of choice. Sam looked embarrassed but pleased at her mother's announcements. (Although it was not necessary in Sam's case, her teacher could have assisted by limiting Sam's discussion of her fears or by offering fun distractions. And if Sam had suffered from a learning problem—luckily, she didn't—accommodations at school would have been high on my priority list.)

Over the next several weeks, family members methodically proceeded to free themselves from Sam's phobias and obsessions. There were occasional flare-ups, mostly temper tantrums at home when Sam didn't get her way, which were handled with time-outs. A larger issue surfaced around this time, one that may have contributed to Sam's problems in the first place: tension between Kathleen and Hank, Sam's biological father. Hank lived nearby, but Sam would get so uncomfortable in the different environment of his home that she would demand to leave. As a result, he saw Sam less than every other weekend. In reality, Kathleen did not trust Hank to take good care of Sam, which I believe was underlying the anxiety that fueled Sam's seemingly haphazard phobias. For his part, Hank was afraid to set limits with Sam, fearing that she would reject him. Katherine and Hank met together with me, and I had Katherine explain Mr. Fear. Hank's supportive reaction allowed Katherine to trust him more, and she explicitly gave Hank her permission to set limits with her daughter. Kathleen pledged to let Sam know that she stood behind Hank's decisions. Over time, Katherine more actively encouraged Sam to spend time with her father.

Although I knew that Sam's sensitivity and intensity made her life difficult, I sincerely believed in her competence, as well as her mother's. All these improvements were accomplished without any medication. Over a three-month period and with this new kind of help from her parents, Sam became a normal little girl. When Katherine believed that Sam was incapacitated by her brain chemistry, she expected very little from her daughter; medication was the only answer for this "broken brain." But when parents proceed with sympathetic expectations of competence and follow through accordingly, their kids improve.

When acting-in behavior carries over to the teen years, parents may be frustrated at the limited assistance they can offer. They can and should reduce their rescuing behaviors, but it's going to be up to the individual teen to take small steps toward competence—steps the parents can reward. In more extreme circumstances, parents may need to be prepared for their child to "hit the wall" with a depression that may require medication or even hospitalization, if the teen is desperate and stuck enough to consider suicidal ideas or actions. Individual therapy for both teens and parents can provide support through these tough times.

Pharmaceutical Interventions

As with acting-out problems, the decision to employ a drug for an inward problem is ultimately an individual choice between family and doctor. The scales are weighted differently, however, because there is much less evidence of the effectiveness and safety of first-line drugs for acting-in problems compared with the ones for the acting-out variety, especially stimulants. To offset the uncertain benefits, as well as the known and unknown risks of medication, a child usually needs to show a high degree of compromised function or disability. Furthermore, there are many therapies, like the one employed with Sam, that are effective for acting-in problems, which should obviously be tried before risks are taken with pharmaceuticals.

The SSRI drugs have become the first line of medication intervention for inward symptoms, some of them proving useful for up to a year for obsessional-type problems in children. Whether they are helpful for other childhood symptoms remains unknown. I would also consider them for teens who appear deeply entrenched in their problem cycle or are at risk for suicide attempts or gestures. Younger children who refuse to leave the house or go to school might also be candidates—but I always caution parents that there is much less evidence that SSRIs offer kids and teens the same degree and frequency of resilience that adults get from the drug. Younger children who fail to improve over a matter of weeks in a focused, parent-assisted behavioral program might also become candidates for an SSRI—but such failure is rare in my practice. Virtually all of the preteens I see are successful without medication.

If one or two different SSRIs don't make enough difference, most doctors employ medications that have been studied primarily for adult depression, possibly offering a newer, "atypical" (meaning the chemical structure is different) antidepressant, like Wellbutrin or Effexor. Sometimes the doctor will use an older tricyclic drug like imipramine (known also by the brand name Tofranil) or nortryptyline (Pamelor). The tricyclics are sedating, so they may be used when insomnia or nighttime symptoms appear.

For anxious children, some doctors add an antianxiety drug like Xanax or Klonopin, usually in combination with an SSRI or antidepressant. Most recommend only short-term or intermittent use of these medications because both tolerance—the need for higher and higher doses—and addiction can develop if these drugs are used for months or even weeks at a stretch. A few physicians prefer Buspar, a non-benzodiazepene antianxiety drug that does not appear to cause addiction; however, many feel it to be neither strong nor effective.

If those medications are not helpful for acting-in type symptoms, other categories of drugs may be used. Parents need to know that they present a higher degree of risk to the child in both the short and the long term. They are rarely prescribed alone; a child who reaches this point may be taking three or more drugs simultaneously. I genuinely question the value of these medications unless the symptoms are life-threatening or completely incapacitating. Difficult questions about the child's problems frequently accompany the decision to use these drugs. Does the child need a special school? Should she remain at home? Is the child's behavior growing more and more bizarre—for example, has she stopped bathing? Beyond the immediate fear, worry, or depression, is the child sounding delusional or psychotic—is a voice or force telling her that her food is poisoned? If there is a threat of suicide, how serious are the suicidal thoughts? Is there a previous history of a suicide attempt? (A previous suicide attempt is the highest risk factor for trying again.)

Lithium and the anticonvulsant class of drugs, including Depakote and Neurontin, may at this point be considered. Some doctors skip these choices and move directly to the novel antipsychotics like Risperdal and Zyprexa, especially if the child shows signs of a psychosis (like visual or auditory hallucinations). Older antipsychotic medications like Mellaril, Haldol, or Thorazine may be tried if these new drugs do not control symptoms. Clozapine (Clozaril) is a unique antipsychotic, rarely used in preteens because of life-threatening side effects. In some teenagers, it may control psychotic behavior when other drugs have failed, but it is often tried last because it requires biweekly blood tests. Stimulants and thyroid hormone drugs will be considered as add-on third, fourth, or fifth medications to "boost" apathetic or depressed behavior.

One nonpharmacological treatment deserves mention here. Some doctors may recommend electroconvulsive therapy (ECT)—electric shocks applied to the head—for older teens who suffer from prolonged and resistant depression. Although ECT is a fairly common "last resort" treatment for depression in adults and especially the elderly, it is rarely used in the United States in teens and never to my knowledge in prepubertal children. ECT is highly controversial, with vigorous proponents who tout its effectiveness and purported safety. But the ethical problem of treating children who do not necessarily have the right to consent to treatment seems an appropriately insurmountable barrier to ECT as an intervention for children's problems.

12

Kids Who Don't Connect with Others

My heart sank silently when I first met Drew, a curly-haired child with dark shadows beneath his coal-black eyes. I had met his parents, Jennifer and Dan, a week earlier. They were pleasant, friendly people who emphasized their nine-year-old son's temper tantrums. He would grow angry over trivial items, sometimes breaking favorite toys. Getting him and his two younger siblings ready and out the door in the morning was a daily grind for Jennifer. Drew had recently made a limited attempt to run away—he was gone for only an hour but his parents were beside themselves with worry before he returned. Tears filled Jennifer's eyes as she spoke: "It's like raising my kids is a jail sentence, a cruel and unusual punishment." For his part, Dan felt both lucky and guilty that he could escape to his Silicon Valley job every day.

I thought that in their descriptions of battles and tantrums, Jennifer and Dan were drawing a picture of your typical oppositional nine-year-old. In retrospect, I should have realized more was going on. Jennifer had mentioned that it wasn't until Drew was six that people outside the family could understand his speech. Even now, he tended to withdraw from conversation unless the subject was Pokémon, with which he was nearly obsessed, according to Jennifer. And Drew—unlike his sociable brother, Ian—rarely had friends visit the house, and he was excluded from the birthday parties and sleepovers typical for kids his age in their community.

When Drew walked into my office for the family visit, he barely greeted me and avoided glancing in my direction. When I asked him his name and age, he answered very quietly, never looking me in the eyes. Even his sitting posture, with his body and face angled away from me, demonstrated his discomfort. From there, he didn't say much at all, unless the subject was Pokémon. His parents had allowed him to bring a binder filled with Pokémon cards, and once he got started describing the characters, he went on and on. The rest of his family listened politely, obviously uninterested but unwilling to interrupt.

Posture, eye contact, taking turns in conversation, nodding the head to indicate attention . . . all these activities are called the *pragmatics of communication*. They're automatic for most of us—we don't give them a thought—but Drew was apparently unaware of, or uncomfortable with, these unspoken "rules" of relating. Any kid who's meeting a stranger and feeling on the spot might withdraw from some of the pragmatics of conversation, and it's always possible that even under the best of circumstances a child is just slow to warm up. But Drew's unease was significant. Later, I'd receive confirmation of how hard it was for him to connect.

By contrast, Ian, Drew's seven-year-old brother, spoke freely and was forthright about what he wanted—to play with the toys. When his parents reminded him to sit with Jennifer on the couch to "talk to the doctor," he stayed long enough to watch Dan put on a puppet show about a moose who would not listen to his mother while getting ready in the morning. Alexis, the youngest child, was yet another extreme. She would not let go of her mother. She sat on Jennifer's lap and, when invited to speak, talked in a baby voice. I knew she was five, but her voice and actions, along with her small size, made her seem closer to three. For his part, Drew was not disruptive, and he seemed to understand the story, but he gazed purposefully away, furtively glancing on occasion toward his father's show.

After the puppet show and a couple of minutes spent playing with separate bins of toys, Drew became interested in Ian's train set. Dan watched from the couch as the boys began to argue; Jennifer, who was playing with a set of dishes with Alexis, looked in the boys' direction but did not say much. The argument escalated to shouts and Ian looked as if he might hit Drew.

"Do you like the way the boys are playing?" I asked. When Jennifer shook her head, I asked her if she could intervene.

"Ian, what's the problem?" she called out.

"Mom, Drew keeps taking that gate and using it for himself. I was playing here first and he came over and now he's hogging stuff!"

"Is that true, Drew?" asked Jennifer.

I felt tension in my chest and was aware that I was quietly sighing. Jennifer was entering the quicksand of trying to determine who's right or wrong when siblings aren't getting along. I expected failure.

"Ian's lying, Mom!" Drew exclaimed with unexpected intensity. "Am not," said Ian instantly.

"Listen, Ian," Jennifer said, as she moved over to inspect the train set-up. "There are two gates. Can't you let Drew have one of them?"

"But mom, I'm using *both* of them." Before the conversation went any further, Drew reached over and grabbed one of the gates. Ian screamed and threw the track he was holding at Drew's tracks. Dan, who had been watching but had otherwise not said much, said sternly and with his voice rising, "Ian, that's not acceptable."

"I don't care. Drew's a dork."

The boys tensely settled into parallel play on the tracks again. Jennifer shrugged and Dan looked at me with a resigned, quizzical look that said, "We've seen this a thousand times and don't know what we can do."

I'd just witnessed demanding, "hogging" behavior from Drew, the kind that had driven his parents to my office for help. (Ian wasn't especially generous, either.) Like kids who act out, he was testing his parents and starting the kinds of battles that other kids do when they're feeling bad or needy. But unlike acting-out children, Drew found it difficult to play the "correct" way. Just as it was a hurdle for

Drew to communicate with his family and me, asking Ian for the gate in a direct, socially appropriate manner appeared to challenge him. He seemed overwhelmed; he might have focused on a thing, the gate, to make him feel safe and comfortable. Drew could definitely be angry, but he was not uncaring, thoughtless, or bad. Nor could his problems be "fixed" easily.

From what I had seen so far, Drew could have met the criteria for a number of psychiatric disorders. Although I am tempted to say that Drew had DSD (Drew-specific disorder), other doctors might diagnose him with one or more of the following conditions: oppositional defiant disorder, generalized anxiety disorder, obsessive-compulsive disorder, pervasive developmental disorder, or Asperger's syndrome. The last two categories are psychiatry's attempt to categorize problems of "relatedness"—connecting to other people.

Most of us have heard of childhood autism. Fully autistic children are on the far end of a relatedness spectrum, one that spans from children who are experts in human social interactions to those who seem to be in a world by themselves. Autistic children relate poorly to people and do not respond to most of the social cues that the rest of us take for granted. They often act strangely, with self-stimulating behavior like twirling about or making whirring or smacking noises with their mouths. If Drew's relatedness problems were magnified by a factor of ten, you'd have a picture of the autistic child.

Although Drew was not autistic, deciphering the reactions of others and responding appropriately was still difficult for him. In 1980, psychiatrists created a category called pervasive developmental disorder (PDD) to account for not just autism but also the part of the relatedness spectrum that includes lesser degrees of trouble. The PDD category turned out to be too broad and nonspecific, and many children with less severe problems were going unrecognized. To correct this gap, the DSM IV (the latest version of the guide, published in 1994) added Asperger's syndrome, a new diagnostic category named after the physician who first described these lesser but still highly problematic patterns of behavior.

Many mental health experts would say that Drew met the criteria for this syndrome. For me, it's less important to say that Drew "has" Asperger's syndrome than to communicate to his parents that Drew's most fundamental and challenging problem is and will be his difficulties relating easily and well to other people. If you can imagine the feeling you get when someone looks directly into your eyes for a prolonged period of time—the feeling that the gaze has become a stare and you need to break away—you have a taste of the strain and pressure that Drew and children like him feel whenever they participate in basic human interactions. Difficulty acquiring and using words in speech and written communication is also often delayed in children with relatedness problems. Although Drew's speech was slow to come, by age nine he'd basically caught up, giving him an advantage compared with severely autistic children, who may have tougher language problems and may also be globally retarded.

As with autism, many of Drew's strangest and most off-putting behaviors are simply his efforts to cope with the stress and difficulty of relating to his family and the outside world. That's demonstrated most clearly in his obsession with Pokémon. The Pokémon world was safe territory for Drew, one in which he could be an expert. Naturally, he tried to direct all conversation to that subject, since other topics, especially those about feelings, were too difficult or threatening. His oppositional behavior could in part be explained by his reluctance to engage with people, and, of course, he was also testing his parents as normal kids do. His intolerance to trivial frustration, his persistence, and his insensitivity to others can all be explained by the stress that his inherent difficulties with relationships engenders.

I saw enough during the first visit to know that Drew and his family were up against multiple challenges, some involving Drew's relatedness problems but others taking in the entire family system. To-

ward the end of our meeting I picked up on some harsh words between the two parents. Jennifer seemed simultaneously tense, depressed, and burned out. Dan had more energy, but he waited a long
time before stepping in to help his wife. During our first encounter,
both parents reported that they were getting along well and seemed
reasonably happy with each other. Now I wasn't as certain and, given
the extent of the problems this family faced, I wasn't surprised.

A phone call to his teacher confirmed my concerns about Drew's
inability to relate to others. He could attract limited peer involvement
with his Pokémon collection, but he generally kept to himself on the
playground. Some of the children complained about his bossiness
when they worked in groups during class.

I was hoping against hope that Drew would look better—that he
would warm up some—during his second visit, but he did not. While
he separated rather easily from his mother to talk and play with me by
himself, once again he showed great difficulty in looking at me directly when we spoke. He looked to the side or down—anywhere but
at me. In an ironic way, he had to be exquisitely aware of just exactly
where I was; only then could he precisely avert his gaze from me.
Conversation between us went a bit better than when his family was
present, but once again he directed our talk to Pokémon. Finally, by
keeping the questions simple and tangible ("Tell me one thing you
like to do at school and one thing you hate to do but must do anyway") I was able to have him speak of other subjects.

At one point, I asked Drew if he would mind looking at me when
he spoke. He immediately looked up and into my eyes for the first
time. I asked him if making eye contact with me was difficult. "Yes,"
he answered, but when I asked him why, he could provide no explanation. He knew that he didn't look at people and was aware it gave
the impression he wasn't interested or didn't care about them. He said
he didn't want people to think that about him. He agreed to try to
look at me when we spoke and said it was okay for me to remind him.

Drew was definitely overwhelmed by social relations, but he had some control over his behavior. Although it wasn't easy, he *could* force himself to look directly at me. Some children would not have been able to look into my eyes at all. To Drew's credit, he also talked about his problems. Again, a more impaired child would have just ignored me or changed the subject. Some might have responded with an odd behavior like flapping their hands like a chicken—a sign of stress called an automatism. In this case, the automatism would be a way of saying, "Don't ask me these questions!" Autistic children rely on automatisms frequently, but Drew used them rarely. In some ways, his milder kind of problem is harder on kids and their parents than outright autism—so much is normal about them that they elicit much less sympathy and receive fewer services.

I noticed another distressing feature about Drew, one that I had missed during the family visit. A couple of times during our twenty-minute attempt at conversation, Drew's eyes twitched for seconds at a time. Once his mouth curled for no apparent reason. Later, when he was relaxing with some of my toys, I heard a series of grunts and whooping noises that were not related to any effort he was making. I wondered whether Drew might, in addition to his relational problems, have a movement disorder that in its most extreme form is called Tourette's syndrome. Most people have heard of Tourette's. The most flagrant sufferers fling their bodies about wildly and shout obscenities for no clear reason, but milder movements like hand-wringing or facial grimaces are more common. One more issue for poor Drew and his parents to deal with, I thought sadly. Drew told me he was aware of the twitches and noises; however, he said that no one ever noticed or complained about them. In fact, his parents had not even mentioned them to me.

Drew's intellectual abilities appeared normal in the office, but later I reviewed testing from the school psychologist. He could easily decode fourth-grade words, but he had difficulty demonstrating that he understood what he had read; he had a similar problem comprehending spoken language. He could mask his struggles in routine conversation about Pokémon, but in tests designed to elicit his strengths and weaknesses, Drew could not explain or at times even remember the nuances of a conversation for the average nine-year-old. On the other hand, Drew was above average in math abilities and superb at analyzing and putting puzzles together. Both skills might prove useful to Drew later in his life, especially in the engineering or mechanical world.

Drew was most severely lacking in a series of abilities that is not assessed on the usual IQ tests given at school, skills called emotional intelligence. Emotional intelligence, popularized by psychologist and journalist Daniel Goleman in the early 1990s, is the ability to read the social reactions of others and respond appropriately. Goleman notes that emotional intelligence is a better predictor of ultimate life happiness than the standard IQ score, which predicts only school success. Goleman also believes that emotional intelligence can be taught and learned, though evidence for training adults in it is weak. Fortunately, there is more hope for children.

Options for Kids with Relatedness Problems

Behavioral Interventions

On rare occasions, an autistic person commands both intelligence and a gift of verbal expression. Temple Grandin, an autistic woman with a Ph.D. in animal husbandry, is such a person; she has become autism's most eloquent spokesperson. Because Grandin lacked the built-in ability to understand human relations—the kind that comes so naturally to most people—she learned how to behave by studying how people act with one another. In his essay on Grandin, the neurologist and writer Oliver Sacks described her as "an anthropologist from Mars," to suggest the quality and immensity of her task.

Grandin credits her parents and an early teacher, all of whom refused to allow her to escape into the self-stimulatory world she preferred, for her success. But even now, Grandin says she understands animals better than humans, and she regularly retreats to a mechanical contraption she created that tightly binds her body. It eases, she says, the sense of being overwhelmed by the demands of relating to people.

Grandin's views are echoed and reinforced by other autistics and the professionals who treat them. That wasn't always the case. As recently as thirty years ago, parents, particularly mothers, were blamed for their children's autistic behavior. Since all children could inherently relate to their mothers, the theory went, these children's difficulties must be caused by "refrigerator mothers" who coldly rejected their kids.

The professional pendulum on the causes of autism has now swung completely to the other side. Although I am generally wary of ascribing behavior purely to one cause or another, my own thinking reflects the mainstream view that much of autism and relatedness problems are inherent, genetic, and biological. Most parents of autistic children are loving mothers and fathers, but the kids reject their parents' earnest attempts at interaction. Raising autistic children has been described as the most thankless of parenting tasks: Parents can pour all their affection and caring into their efforts and still receive nothing in kind back from their children.

If Drew's behavior was no longer considered the fault of parenting or environment, but solely a genetic problem, what then could be done about it? Grandin's impression—that she was helped by not being allowed to escape into her own world—coincides with the direction of professional interventions in the 1990s. They offer the first new ray of hope for autistic children. Called discrete reinforcement training by some and the Lovass approach (after the UCLA researcher, Ivar Lovass) by others, children identified at young ages as autistic undergo an intense, massive behavioral modification program in their homes and at school.

The goal is to reinforce socially appropriate behavior and ignore or punish autistic or avoidant behavior. Professional trainers come to the home for up to six hours a day, work with the child, and teach parents the techniques. The training is rigorous and difficult on the parents and the child. It has been called "kiddie boot camp," and its use of food rewards strikes some as distastefully similar to dog-obedience school, but it works. Up to 90 percent of the children who never listened to a "no" learn to respond to limits, and between one and two out of ten autistic children appear normal after two years of decreasingly intense treatment.

Another school of intervention, called "floor time," has been promoted by Stanley Greenspan, a respected researcher. In this approach, parents get down on the floor with their child and join in the child's activity. If the child is simply banging a toy truck against the wall, the parent bangs the truck too. The parent then introduces a new element of interaction, perhaps removing the truck from the child's hand and rolling it along the floor, saying "zoom." Over time, the interactions ideally grow more complex. Although it is fine for parents to try floor time, most children flee from the interaction without the additional rewards and punishments of discrete reinforcement training.

Drew did not require this kind of full-on intervention, but I felt he would benefit from a similar approach, scaled down for his milder level of difficulty. Instead of professional trainers, his parents would be the ones to keep Drew from escaping social interaction: "Drew, we'll talk about Pokémon later, but first I want to discuss this story we've read." Rewards could help too: "If we can talk about the story for five minutes, I'll give you a star good toward candy after dinner. And then we can talk about Pokémon."

Pharmaceutical Interventions

Most professionals are willing to consider medication for kids with relatedness problems, especially when behavioral interventions don't work or aren't available. But parents hoping for a pharmaceutical "cure" need to be realistic. Although various psychiatric drugs have been tried over the years, none of them actually address the core difficulty associated with autism, PDD, or Asperger's. The medications that doctors use are intended for the *complications* of relatedness problems, not the problem itself. A child like Drew, who suffers from learning disabilities, might reasonably be given a stimulant to help him stick with challenging or boring tasks at school. For irritability, tantrums, or self-stimulatory behaviors—which are thought to be connected to anxiety—a doctor might prescribe an SSRI like Prozac or Zoloft. There is no proof that SSRIs help, but sometimes a child's behavior is so distressing that a trial seems justified.

When these drugs (in combination, one hopes, with behavioral interventions) do not provide sufficient assistance, a doctor and family may choose to try second-line medications. Which ones depends on the child's most difficult behaviors. Clonidine or Tenex, for example, might be added to a stimulant to control oppositional behavior, especially in the evening hours. Such a decision is not to be made lightly, as these drugs can have more serious side effects, especially in combination with others.

Severely autistic children often wind up on end-of-the-line medications. These kids are *not* the ones with Asperger's or more moderate relatedness problems. They are at the extreme end of the range, are often severely developmentally delayed, and can challenge their caregivers with highly aggressive behavior (hitting, biting, and so on). They may also retreat into self-stimulatory habits, even going so far as to hurt themselves (banging their heads or biting and chewing their own arms and legs) as a means of coping with the demands of socialization. Some of these drugs have been tested on children with autism—the antipsychotic medications may be more likely to contain the bizarre and challenging behaviors of these children. Anticonvulsants or lithium may be tried as well.

All these drugs are characterized by serious and regular side effects, but I appreciate that parents who try them are faced with equally wrenching alternatives, often involving placement of the child in a special school or home. I wish that more families of autistic children had the opportunity to participate fully in a discrete behavioral reinforcement treatment plan. Perhaps only one in ten autistic children achieves normalcy with this approach, but the nine out of ten children who learn to respond to a verbal "no" are far less likely to need medication.

OPTIONS FOR TICS

People with physical or verbal tics compare them to the cough that sometimes follows an upper respiratory infection: You feel a tickle in your throat and, no matter how hard you try, you can suppress the cough only for so long. If you're lucky, you can find a secluded place before the cough bursts forth. But five minutes later, you feel the tickle again.

The twitches and vocalizations of Tourette's syndrome often accompany behavioral problems (and vice versa) and are not dangerous in themselves. Most of the movements appear to wax and wane according to the child's stress level. Often they increase during the adolescent years but begin to fade away in the twenties. But tics like Drew's can elicit hurtful reactions from other people, who may tease him or freeze him out for being "weird." Since Drew's parents were not bothered by the tics and his schoolmates apparently had not made any comments, I was not inclined to treat them with medication. But if he had experienced a negative social reaction, I would have been ready to offer medication that has been shown to help. Clonidine or Tenex is usually tried first; if unsuccessful, the next choice is usually a low-dose prescription for an antipsychotic like Haldol. Although nondrug approaches like biofeedback and meditation, which help people handle stress, might have some appeal for Tourette's, no studies have been published in major journals proving their effectiveness for this use.

"Pure Hell"

Children like Drew, whose problems are not as severe as those at the autistic range of the scale, can fall between the cracks. Not only had Drew come to me relatively late in his development, but his family had so many other problems—some as a consequence of Drew's behavior—that the creation of a coherent effective intervention for Drew posed great challenges.

Almost immediately after I met Drew and his family, they plunged into a crisis. They came on the Monday after a weekend that the parents described as "pure hell." Drew went to a classmate's poorly supervised birthday party and missed out on receiving a prize at the end. He had a major temper tantrum at home. Only after his parents repeatedly screamed at him did his anger break, and then he cried for several hours. Jennifer looked drawn and sounded despondent. She said she was exhausted—and acknowledged she had been taking Zoloft for the last six months. Jennifer said it was helping her cope somewhat and told me that she thought Drew needed medication, something to assist him *right now.*

I honestly didn't know who needed relief more, mother or son. I might have offered medication to Jennifer first, but since she was already taking Zoloft, I felt stuck. I knew that the family was desperate. I floated the idea of sending Drew to a relative for a week, to give them all a break, but there was no one who could take him.

This family needed much more than medication for Drew. The other children's behavior and the relationship between Jennifer and Dan called out for a systemic solution that would include counseling, especially for the parents. But if I didn't provide some form of quick, short-term help, I was likely to lose this family entirely and miss the opportunity to help them.

We decided that Drew would try Zoloft, initially at the lowest dose available, and agreed that if there was no change in his behavior or mood after about a week, his parents could increase the dose. Jennifer and Dan were aware that there was little to no data that Zoloft would help Drew and that there was no long-term safety track record for this medication when used in Drew's age-group. However, like many families in this situation, the parents were willing to take risks in the hope that the medication could give them some immediate relief. Drew was unhappy enough at the moment—he could be genuinely regretful over the trouble he caused his parents—to agree to try the medication.

We also talked through some behavioral interventions. Once again, I focused on getting the parents to become more effective disciplinarians. With some effort on my part, Jennifer and Dan—who had different standards for their kids—were able to agree on some basic rules, like no hitting or spitting. All those involved in that interaction would immediately go to time-out.

The family was better at our meeting a week later. As usual, it was hard to ascribe a specific cause: Maybe the kids had just settled down, or the parents were a bit more effective, or the medication had eased Drew's irritability and mood. He definitely had fewer tantrums than the previous week, and the parents expressed a desire to work on getting their kids ready in the morning with less fussing. When they left, both Jennifer and Dan seemed enthusiastic about the clothes-in-the-bag approach to getting ready in the mornings that I described in Chapter 4.

However, they never employed the technique. When they came to see me the next week, Drew seemed a bit better, but Ian was completely out of control. Jennifer looked disconsolate as Dan announced he'd been laid off from his high-tech job due to industry cutbacks. I was worried that Dan didn't seem to appreciate how depressed and angry his wife was. Jennifer deflected my efforts to acknowledge her situation and instead wanted me to focus on the children. We talked about how Ian, not just Drew, needed limits, and planned a next visit for just the parents.

They did not return. I called the family twice, but they did not return my messages. I spoke to their pediatrician, sharing my observations and worries about the family, and pondered whether I had done anything wrong. In retrospect, perhaps Jennifer and Dan found my focus on her unhappiness too threatening. I think she may have felt that I was blaming her. Or perhaps the parents feared that in meeting with me their marital problems—which were becoming more and more obvious—would break undeniably into the open. Possibly Dan's unemployment deprived them of the funds necessary to continue. Or maybe they had what they wanted: a prescription for Drew. But their not returning my calls suggests that I blew it with them.

Drew's developmental and personality problems, in combination with family tension, are a common double whammy. Deciding what to address first is sometimes difficult. Medication can be helpful for both the parents and children. But in Drew's case, the fundamental problems with relatedness and language comprehension have no clear medical answers. Typically, doctors are left with attempting to ameliorate the associated symptoms that develop with these types of core problems.

Drew would have benefited from coherent and organized behavioral treatment when he was younger. But he could still make gains in dealing with people if properly reinforced. Ian, without any social awkwardness, could also benefit from increased consistency of discipline and rewards for good behavior, and Alexis could be encouraged to conduct herself in a manner appropriate to her age ("We don't answer to baby talk," her parents could tell her, kindly). Whether Jennifer and Dan, in their own compromised state, could provide the level of consistent, confident parenting demanded by their challenging children is questionable. It's hard to say for sure where Drew is heading, but his inherent problems, along with his family's struggles, make him a likely candidate for more psychiatric medication in the future.

PART THREE

*Beyond Diagnosis
and Drugs*

13

Toward a Moral Treatment of Behavior Problems in Children

Pippi Longstocking just left my office on Ritalin. Of course, that's not her real name. Her name could be Kayley, Anna, Natalie, or that of a half dozen other girls I saw this week.

According to her teacher, eleven-year-old "Pippi" was not performing up to her potential at her private school. She daydreamed in class and often was not prepared to answer when called on. She could be silly in the classroom. In my office, however, this girl demonstrated academic skills that were two grade levels above average. She spoke to me cogently and thoughtfully about her life. She dreamed about living on a ranch with many animals. She acted a bit nervous and giggly when she was with her parents and her more serious younger brother. But she did not seem to present a serious case of hyperactivity or inattentiveness, and I told her parents so. I suggested that we work on making consequences more immediate for Pippi at home and at school; if she had not sufficiently improved in a few months, perhaps Ritalin could be tried then.

Pippi's mom asked me if there was really anything bad about taking Ritalin. If not, why couldn't I prescribe now, so that Pippi could do better in school immediately? I explained that most children and adults have little problem taking Ritalin and that it was probably safe.

Pippi's dad, uneasy about using a drug that also had abuse potential, decided that they should wait.

The family came back to see me a week later. Dad had changed his mind. Another doctor felt that Pippi had mild ADHD and gave them a prescription—but had left them with no instructions beyond following the information printed on the label. Pippi apparently felt okay about taking it. Although I had made it clear that I did not think she needed medication at this time, the family asked me if I would tell them more about how to use the drug. I showed them how to titrate the optimal dose and frequency and provided them a feedback sheet they could give to the teacher. They left happy. I felt strange.

I find myself evaluating more and more Pippis and Tom Sawyers for medication these days. These seemingly normal children are often inattentive or uninterested in school and a bit slow to finish their chores at home. Concerned and loving parents bring them in because the children are not "performing up to their potential" or are disruptive in their classrooms. Debate over medicating these kids continues to develop white heat and light, most prominently in stories that appear in national and local media.

An article that appeared in the February 2000 issue of the *Journal of the American Medical Association* reported a 500 percent increase between 1990 and 1995 in the use of stimulant drugs in children aged three to five. The statistic made front-page headlines and so alarmed the country that two national scientific conferences were organized to address the toddlers-on-Ritalin question. Even the first lady at the time, Hillary Clinton, raised her voice in cautious alarm. The news had people asking, Just what constitutes abnormal behavior in this normally boisterous age-group? How can medications be justified when there is virtually no research on the effectiveness and safety of psychoactive drugs for younger children? Both are excellent questions that apply to many kids on psychiatric medication, whether they have been diagnosed with ADHD or some other problem.

Later in 2000, another headline-making story captured the plight
of two families in the Albany, New York, area. They had been referred
to the family courts, accused of child neglect when they decided to
stop giving their kids psychiatric drugs. In both cases, the children's
schools told the local child protective service agency that the children's behavior—in the opinion of school personnel—necessitated
the medication (stimulants in both cases; one child was also taking
Prozac). Both families felt that the medications were not helpful or
were causing unacceptable side effects. The family court judges de-
clined to take the children away from the parents, and alternative solutions were found.

Despite this apparently happy ending, the cases highlight how far
our culture has come in believing that child behavior problems are
medical disorders requiring medical interventions. They also show
just how far a school system may go in pressuring parents to medicate
their child. This pressure is perceived as so pervasive and ubiquitous
that it has led to congressional investigations (at one of which I testified). A few state legislatures have passed laws reminding teachers
that they first must exhaust educational and disciplinary remedies before suggesting a medical evaluation for a school problem. Many
more states are considering similar actions. Some have viewed these
efforts as clumsy, cudgel-like "gag" laws, but I see them more as a
frightened reaction from those elements of the society who are uncomfortable with social agencies dictating a medication solution.

What is sickness, anyway? What is normal for a child—and what
is above or below average? Such broad questions seem pertinent, not
just to the role of physicians in general but also to my situation as a
doctor treating children's behavioral and performance problems in the
new American millennium. I already know that there are no clear answers or standards. In 1996 I attended a conference of ethicists, the-
ologians, judges, physicians, and psychologists—a supposedly ideal
environment for our goal of, among other things, addressing the line
between treatment (of the sick) and enhancement (of the well or nor-

mal). But no one could agree on just where or even how that line should be located. However, a few things are clear to me. If such a line exists, it isn't fixed. It's blurry from constant motion, and it's nearly always culturally or socially determined.

I might try the question from another angle: Which is it that causes sickness and health, function and dysfunction—nature or nurture? But this query sets up a false dichotomy; it denies the ongoing interaction between both nature and nurture in the growing child. Where one influence begins and the other reacts is often unclear. Do environmental factors affect sperm and eggs? Radiation certainly does. Can the intrauterine environment influence a fetus? Absolutely. But the newborn child also possesses genes, a template of talents and temperament. These traits are there from the beginning, directing the infant's behavior—which can then profoundly influence the behavior of the parents. In their turn, parents, school, and society influence the child. Theoretical attempts to prove that either nature or nurture is predominant seem more reflective of the current needs and prerogatives of culture and society than of the "science" involved. Yet the Albany cases demonstrate the allure and power of the belief that behavior is determined solely by biochemistry.

I try to keep these philosophical Mobius strips in mind when considering the role of doctors and psychiatrists in helping troubled kids. Culturally, my job as a behavioral pediatrician and family therapist is to ease suffering. Some might say that this goal is accomplished by helping people "fit in," to smooth some of the rougher edges between individual personalities and their societies. But the psychiatrist Thomas Szasz has persistently challenged this approach to doctoring and psychiatry, pointing out that the "insane" or "dysfunctional" person may actually be responding in a sensible and functional manner to an environment that is itself oppressive or even crazy. What constitutes "normal" may sometimes be oppressive to the individual or destructive to the culture. Physicians and psychiatrists must take a comprehensive approach to easing suffering, one that does not reduce the task to briskly treating the symptoms and getting people back to work.

Szasz's concerns remain relevant whenever medication is prescribed. Are we simply getting a person who has an understandable response to a bad situation to quiet down and fit in? When we are addressing "disorders" that affect groups with less social power—like children—these questions take on special resonance. Robert Coles, the child psychiatrist and moralist, adds his own concerns:

> These days, more and more, psychiatrists think of their patients as neurochemically unbalanced in one way or another, as challenges, therefore, to a gradual process of drug initiation and titration. A growing number of patients spend little or no time talking with their doctors about the everyday difficulties in getting through life; rather, they hope for a kind of calm to settle on them, courtesy of a pill that will do its work, cast its magic spell by dint of its effect on the brain's circuitry.

An opposing voice in this debate comes from Gerald L. Klerman, who articulated the concept of "pharmacological Calvinism." While working as a research psychiatrist at Columbia in the 1970s, Klerman challenged the notion that improvement by using one's own resources or through the joint effort of psychotherapy was somehow morally superior to improvement achieved by taking a pill. He wondered whether time and money spent on therapy could be justified when a drug could produce the same result more quickly and cheaply.

Not only does Klerman's point of view skirt the issues raised by Szasz and Coles, it becomes even more problematic when considering the treatment of children. We must be prepared to set the ethical bar for treatment of children higher than we do for adults. Children rarely make the decision to seek or obtain treatment for themselves. Except in rare situations, children have no legal say over their treatment. And there is the physician's dictum of *primum non nocere*—first, do no harm. To be sure, the absence of medical treatment can sometimes carry its own risks. But we still don't know for sure if any of these drugs make a difference over the long run (and for most of these drugs, even the short-term benefits for kids are unknown). Even when a pill "works" and improves a child's behavior or performance, it is not the moral equivalent of helping parents become better parents and helping teachers teach.

That's why I believe that the evaluation and treatment of children is neither complete nor ethical unless it looks beyond the symptoms, to the fullest possible understanding of a child's brain and behavior within the context of that child's world. I believe in multi-visit evaluations that include the entire family, and I emphasize the need for fathers as well as mothers to get involved from the very beginning. I believe that doctors should communicate with the school directly, both to receive another perspective on the child's behavior and to advocate for any classroom changes they feel can be useful. I encourage parents to move away from seeing their child as "disordered." I ask them to seek out examples of competence in their child and hold her to reasonable standards. I ask them to provide a secure, stable home environment in which rules and limits are enforced with loving strength. And I try to be there for parents and children, who may need an anchor as they wait out the sometimes stormy process of growing up.

But it may be difficult to find a physician who employs this deliberate, more considered approach. Although some simply disagree because of ideology or training, the main reason professionals avoid a complete, ethical treatment is dollars and cents. Unfortunately, the care of children is not necessarily an asset to the quarterly bottom line of a family, a medical practice, or even our institutions and corporations. A short evaluation based on counting symptoms and doling out pills is much faster and cheaper—at least in the short term. At least one prominent physician, Joseph Biederman at Harvard, has echoed Klerman's stance where ADHD is concerned. As a nation, he claims, we simply cannot afford the costs of the psychosocial treatments that work for kids who "have" this disorder.

In response, I offer a Swiftian "modest proposal." Based on numbers from the year 2000, there are approximately 4 million children taking stimulants in America, with classroom size averaging twenty-nine children. To save money, I propose we increase the number of children taking stimulants to 7 million. Why not? We could probably increase class size to forty-five kids, reducing taxpayers' burdens and making life easier for kids, educators, parents, and the general public.

The challenge for America in the twenty-first century is to decide how far we want to let the efficiencies and amorality of the marketplace guide our choices about our children. Do we want to streamline child rearing as we have streamlined corporations, turning to drugs to make the job easier and less time-consuming? The mark of a civilized society is how it treats its powerless and weak. And when we use drugs to try to solve our problems, we do so at our own peril.

Although politics, society, and money impinge on nearly every aspect of evaluation and treatment, they are usually out of the immediate control of the parents and doctors who are seeking help for an individual child. But I find that everyone involved in the process welcomes an overt acknowledgment of the social factors. Parents and teachers appreciate the opportunity to speak about work schedules, long commutes, the overvaluation of material acquisitions, the new and increased demands on children to learn earlier and faster, and the financial pressures on schools and administrators. I know *I* do. Such a discussion reminds us that our endeavors take place within a larger framework. I like to spend a little time noting with parents how much more we ask of children these days. When they fail to perform to our higher standards of behavior or academic performance, adults may get anxious and want to fix their children. Our society could benefit from a deep collective sigh—while recognizing that the greatest problems facing America's children continue to be poverty, violence, and racism.

Medicating children is not an either/or choice for a culture. On a pragmatic level, a small number of kids would have trouble finding a good fit, no matter what the family, school, or society. One possible environmental approach—placing the child in an institutional setting—is accompanied by its own serious limitations. Medication that allows these children to "fit in" a little better could make moral sense. But the vast majority of kids taking psychiatric medication in this country are nowhere near this severely affected. Often they are more like the girl mentioned at the beginning of this chapter. Currently, our country has an intolerance for temperamental diversity in our children. I worry about an America where there's no place for an unmedicated Pippi Longstocking or Tom Sawyer.

Since I do medicate children, I also feel obliged to speak out about today's larger social and economic pressures. Children, parents, and teachers are in the grip of a vise, asked to produce more in terms of behavior and performance; at the same time, they are offered less and less support. To prescribe drugs and not attempt to make changes in the larger environment would make me complicit with the values and influences I think are harmful to children—so I continue to speak out, even as I continue to medicate.

American society continues to face the question of how it wants to address the problems of children. The evidence in the near term says that we have decided to "fix" children's brains rather than examine and change their environments. We must question and challenge this choice until we, as a society, experience a fundamental change in our values and beliefs—a change that will restore the acceptance of human diversity and the importance of nurture and care in the raising of our children.

A Quick Guide to the Psychiatric Drugs Most Commonly Prescribed for Children

This guide is a directory of the drugs most commonly prescribed for children's behavioral and emotional problems. It is intended to answer requests from parents for an easy-to-use reference, one that sifts through the staggering—sometimes paralyzing—quantity of information available in professional guides like the *Physician's Desk Reference*.

The drugs are listed by class, starting with the best-known and most popular and moving on to those used less frequently. The problems for which the class of drugs is used, the most frequent or most significant side effects, and dosing information are included, sometimes with comments about controversies or other details of which parents should be aware. Then comes a list of brand-name drugs within each class—again, starting with the best-known or most popular—so that you can look up specifics about a given medication, such as side effects and dosing considerations that are particular to that preparation.

Keeping parents' requests in mind, I have made this guide complete but not exhaustive. For example, I omit drugs that are used very rarely and include only the most salient information in the entries. If you are looking for more information, you may wish to consult Chapter 8, which features an expanded discussion of psychoactive drugs. Ultimately, your best reference is a trusted and experienced doctor.

Stimulants

Prescribed for: Acting-out behavior; impulsivity; inattention; hyperactivity (ADHD); but also for oppositional and defiant behavior (ODD). **Side effects:** Decreased appetite; trouble falling asleep; muscle tics (disputed); growth delay (disputed). **Dosing information:** Lowest dose available is given to start; increased by one tablet every 3 to 4 days, depending on feedback from child/par-

223

ents/teacher, until optimal behavior and performance are reached and/or significant side effects occur. Because length of action—how long the drug works—is often the determining factor in which drug is taken, variations within brand names (such as Ritalin, Ritalin SR, and Ritalin LA) are each given separate consideration below. **Comments:** Effects are nonspecific (low-dose stimulants will improve nearly anyone's focus on tasks that are boring or difficult); onset of action is 20 to 30 minutes; drug abuse potential for teens and adults.

Preparations

Ritalin (methylphenidate).   **Available in:** 5, 10, 20 mg tablets. **Dosing information:** Length of action is 3 to 4 hours. **Comments:** Most widely known stimulant; generic is as good as brand name.

Dexedrine (dextroamphetamine).   **Available in:** 5 mg scored tablet. **Dosing information:** Length of action is 3 to 6 hours. **Comments:** Amphetamine is somewhat more intense than methylphenidate; slightly higher rates of side effects.

Dexedrine Spansule (dextroamphetamine).   **Available in:** 5, 10, 15 mg capsules. **Dosing information:** Length of action is 6 to 8 hours. **Comments:** Action is more consistently sustained than that of Adderall.

Dextrostat (dextroamphetamine).   **Available in:** 5, 10 mg tablets. **Dosing information:** See Dexedrine.

Ritalin SR (methylphenidate).   **Available in:** 20 mg tablets. **Dosing information:** Length of action is 6 to 8 hours. **Comments:** Manufacturer's claim of duration of action disputed by many doctors.

Adderall (amphetamine salts).   **Available in:** 5, 7.5, 10, 12.5, 15, 20, 30 mg scored tablets. **Dosing information:** Length of action is 3 to 8 hours. **Comments:** Duration of action varies considerably among individuals. See Dexedrine.

Methyllin ER (methylphenidate).   **Available in:** 10, 20 mg tablets. **Dosing information:** Length of action is 6 to 8 hours. **Comments:** To date, experience with this preparation is limited.

Metadate ER (methylphenidate).   **Available in:** 10, 20 mg tablets. **Dosing information:** Length of action is 6 to 8 hours. **Comments:** Appears to deliver length of action consistently.

Concerta (methylphenidate).   **Available in:** 18, 36, 54 mg tablets. **Dosing information:** Length of action is 10 to 12 hours. **Comments:** Effective once-a-day preparation; cannot be crushed to swallow; longer action can lead to more sleep problems.

Metadate CD (methylphenidate).   **Available in:** 20 mg capsules. **Dosing information:** Length of action is 10 to 12 hours. **Comments:** Too new to evaluate manufacturer's claims regarding length of action; cannot be crushed to swallow.

Adderall XR (amphetamine salts).   **Available in:** 10, 20, 30 mg capsules. **Dosing information:** Length of action is 10 to 12 hours. **Comments:** Too new to evaluate manufacturer's claims regarding length of action; cannot be crushed to swallow.

Ritalin LA (methylphenidate).   **Dosing information:** Lasts 10 to 12 hours, according to the manufacturer. **Comments:** Just released; too new to evaluate.

Focalin (refined single isomer d-methylphenidate).   **Available in:** 2.5, 5, 10 mg tablets. **Dosing information:** Lasts 3 to 4 hours. **Comments:** Just released; dosages recommended by manufacturer are half those of regular Ritalin (methylphenidate), but the advantages of this preparation are not clear at all.

Cylert (pemoline).   **Available in:** 18.75, 37.5, 75 mg grooved tablets; 37.5 mg chewable tablets. **Dosing information:** Once-a-day dosing. **Comments:** Different structure and action from rest of stimulant class; reports of death from liver failure have led to rare use.

Selective Serotonin Reuptake Inhibitors (SSRIs)

Prescribed for: Increased resilience and improvement of mood; SSRIs specifically decrease anxiety, worries, obsession, and compulsion; may improve depression and agitation in children (not as effectively nor consistently as with adults). **Side effects:** May initially cause sleeplessness, but daytime drowsiness/spaciness is also reported; high rates of sexual side effects (trouble with ejaculation, climax, decreased libido) reported in adults, with unclear implications for children or teens; rare agitation and/or bizarre behavioral reactions. **Dosing information:** For preteens, half of lowest dose available is given to start; teens may begin on full tablet. Dosage is increased by one-half or full tablet every 2 to 4 weeks, depending on response and/or occurrence of side effects; higher dosages generally no greater than twice the usual adult starting dose (e.g., for Prozac, not higher than 40 mg); many SSRIs now available in liquid form, making them easier to use with small children. **Comments:** Despite widespread pediatric use, these medications have not been well studied in children, with no long-term data for safety or effectiveness. Differences among drugs of this class are small, except for length of action; specifically, the effects of Prozac (fluoxetine) will last for several weeks if discontinued. There are some differences in stimulation versus sedation between SSRIs; Prozac is the most stimulatory, Paxil the most sedating. For all SSRIs, onset of action is said to be 2 to 4 weeks but effects are often reported within 2 to 3 days.

Preparations

Prozac (fluoxetine).   **Available in:** 10, 20, 40 mg capsules; 10 mg scored tablet (can be divided); 20 mg/tsp mint-flavored suspension. **Comments:** Best-known of the SSRIs, but not substantially different from the others except for length of action; preferred if "forgetting" to take medication is a problem (take two the next day when one is skipped); avoid if there are major concerns about side effects, since they may linger for weeks even after stopping the drug. Prozac is the only SSRI currently available in a less expensive generic version.

Zoloft (sertraline). **Available in:** 25, 50, 100 mg scored tablets. **Dosing information:** Can be given twice a day to minimize side effects. **Comments:** Data supports effectiveness for childhood OCD-type symptoms for as long as a year; may be slightly less stimulatory than Prozac.

Paxil (paroxetine). **Available in:** 10, 20, mg tablets; 30, 40 mg scored tablets; 10mg/tsp orange-flavored suspension. **Comments**: Requires daily dosing, usually in A.M.

Luvox (fluvoxamine). **Available in:** 25 mg tablets; 50, 100 mg scored tablets. **Comments:** Data supports use in pediatric OCD; Luvox is the most sedating of the SSRIs; useful for nighttime if sleeping is a problem.

Celexa (citalopram). **Available in:** 20, 40 mg scored tablets; 10 mg/tsp peppermint-flavored solution. **Comments:** Taken daily in A.M.; Celexa is a newer SSRI, often tried as a second choice if another SSRI has failed.

Antipsychotics

Prescribed for: Mostly as a last resort for oppositional, angry, aggressive, violent, and out-of-control behavior; also for alleviation of hallucinations and disordered thinking of psychosis; used in low doses for control of extreme anxiety and Tourette's syndrome. **Side effects:** Varies somewhat with drug used; sedation (less common with the newer "atypical" antipsychotics); weight gain (especially common); dry mouth; blurred vision; constipation; increased heart rate; muscle tightness and spasm with long-term use; sense of restlessness (akathesia) and a Parkinson's disease-like condition with hand tremor; general slowness and flat facial affect; neuroleptic malignant syndrome, characterized by muscle spasms, confusion, and high fever (very rare but life-threatening); with long-term use, development of permanent muscle movement disorder called tardive dyskinesia. **Dosing information:** Varies according to drug (see below for specifics); generally, lowest dosage available is given but can be increased rapidly (daily) to achieve control of symptoms. **Comments**: Benadryl (diphenhydramine) or Cogentin (amantadine) may be prescribed along with some of the antipsychotics to prevent or ameliorate some side effects. Some antipsychotic preparations are known as "atypical" or "novel," as they as structurally different from the previous generation of medications.

Preparations

Risperdal (risperidone). **Available in:** 0.25, 0.5, 1, 2, 3, 4 mg tablets; 1 mg/1 cc oral solution with dispensing calibrated pipette. **Dosing information:** Usually given once or twice a day. **Side effects:** Risperdal is the most widely used of the newer generation "atypical" or "novel" antipsychotics, popular because of allegedly less sedation and less risk of tardive dyskinesia with long-term use. Recent data indicates risk of tardive dyskinesia may be the same for those using an antipsychotic for the first time; massive ("Pickwickian") weight gain can occur with continuing use.

Zyprexa (olanzapine).   **Available in:** 2.5, 5, 7.5, 10 mg tablets; 5, 10 mg "orally disintegrating" tablets. **Dosing information:** Usually dosage is once a day. **Side effects:** Allegedly less weight gain than with Risperdal but no evidence for this claim; as with other "atypical" antipsychotics, claims of less sedation and tardive dyskinesia.

Seroquel (quetiapine).   **Available in:** 25, 100, 200 mg tablets. **Dosing information:** Usually prescribed twice or three times a day. **Comments:** One of the newer "atypical" antipsychotics; likely to be a third- or fourth-choice drug; less weight gain but too new to be certain.

Geodon (ziprasidone).   **Available in:** 20, 40, 60, 80 mg capsules. **Dosing information:** Once daily. **Comments:** Newest of "atypical" antipsychotics. The lowest dose available is high for children, who may become sedated.

Clozaril (clozapine).   **Available in:** 25, 100 scored tablets. **Prescribed for:** Generally the ultimate last resort for drug-resistant schizophrenia. **Side effects:** Relatively high risk of agranulocytosis, a potentially fatal blood disorder. **Dosing information:** Manufacturer requires blood counts every other week to prevent the occurrence of blood side effects. **Comments:** Generally not used for children or teenagers because of the need for frequent blood monitoring and relatively high risk of dangerous side effects.

Haldol (haloperidol).   **Available in:** 0.5, 1, 2, 5, 10, 20 mg scored tablets; 2mg/ml flavorless suspension. **Side effects:** Relatively more side effects than with "atypical" antipsychotics like Risperdal. **Dosing information:** Usually given twice a day, sometimes three times a day. **Comments:** Haldol has been a mainstay antipsychotic treatment for many years; used in low doses for effective control of tics in Tourette's syndrome (tends not to be associated with tardive dyskinesia when used for this indication); much less expensive than the "atypical" antipsychotics.

Mellaril (thioridazine).   **Available in:** 10, 15, 25, 50, 100, 200 mg tablets; 5, 6, 20 mg/tsp suspension. **Side effects:** See Haldol. **Dosing information:** Given two or three times daily. **Comments:** Another long-term mainstay for the control of very difficult behavior in children; also less expensive than the "atypical" antipsychotics.

Thorazine (chlorpromazine).   **Available in:** 10, 25, 50, 100, 200 mg tablets and spansules; 10 mg/tsp syrup; 25, 100 mg suppositories. **Side effects:** See Haldol. **Dosing information:** Two or three times daily. **Comments:** The granddaddy of antipsychotic drugs; accidental discovery of Thorazine's antipsychotic properties in the 1950s ushered in the "biological" revolution in psychiatry.

Anticonvulsants

Prescribed for: "Mood disorders," specifically bipolar disorder, but widely used nonspecifically for control of extreme irritability, aggression, and anger. **Side effects:** All these drugs share sedation as the most common limiting side effect; other side effects, some serious, vary according to individual drug as listed below. **Comments:** Anticonvulsants—drugs used in the treatment of epilepsy—have a long history of being employed on occasion for psychiatric use. With the increased willingness to employ psychiatric drugs in children and the widespread rise in the bipolar diagnosis, some of these drugs are prescribed frequently to children with behavioral and emotional problems. Given the lack of supporting data of effectiveness and safety for use in children's psychiatric problems, the widespread use of the anticonvulsants is astonishing and worrisome. Recently, many doctors have been skipping this class of medicines entirely and using the newer antipsychotic medicines for the treatment of extreme acting-out behaviors.

Preparations

Depakote (valproic acid; Valproate/Depakene sprinkles). **Available in:** 125, 250, 500 mg tablets or capsules; 500 mg extended release (ER) tablets; 250 mg/tsp suspension. **Side effects:** Sedation (common); dizziness; nausea; weight loss or gain; development of ovarian cysts and polycystic ovarian disease reported in teenage girls; rare reversible inflammation of the liver (chemical hepatitis); rare but potentially fatal hemorrhagic pancreatitis; decrease in white blood cells with rare but potentially fatal leukemia. **Dosing information:** Lowest dose is given twice daily and increased every two weeks until behavior improves or side effects occur; there are accepted levels of drug in the blood for the control of seizures, but clinical response determines dose for psychiatric problems. **Comments**: ER preparation allows for once-a-day dosing.

Neurontin (gabapentin). **Available in:** 100, 300, 400, 600, 800 mg capsules or tablets. **Side effects:** Possibly less sedation than Depakote; dizziness. **Dosing information:** No established dosing schedule for children; advisable for doctor to begin with 100 mg three times daily, increasing dose every several weeks until behavior improves or side effects (usually sedation) occur. **Comments:** Used increasingly for severe anxiety; Neurontin is newer than Depakote with supposedly fewer side effects; its benefits are unproven, only time will tell.

Tegretol (carbamazepine). **Available in:** 100 mg chewable tablets; 200 mg scored tablets; 100, 200, 400 extended-release (XR) tablets; 100 mg/tsp vanilla-orange-flavored suspension. **Side effects:** Stomach upset (recommended that Tegretol be taken with food); sedation; nausea; vomiting; blurred vision; rare chemical hepatitis or fatal anemia (premedication and regular laboratory blood tests to monitor liver functions and blood count are recommended). **Dosing in-**

formation: Generally, 200 mg is a total daily starting dose, either divided twice a day or once a day as an XR tablet; blood levels are available to guide dosing but clinical response or occurrence of side effects is more important. **Comments:** Tegretol is a mainstay medication for the control of children's seizures; it is less frequently prescribed than Depakote for childhood psychiatric problems because of side effects and perhaps less effectiveness.

Lamictal (lamotrigine).   **Available in:** 25, 50, 150, 200 mg scored tablets; 5, 25 mg chewable tablets. **Side effects:** Skin rashes common, including rare but potentially fatal complication of Stevens-Johnson syndrome, which mimics severe burn injuries. **Comments:** Newer anticonvulsant, now being used for childhood psychiatric problems; likely a third- or fourth-choice medication.

Topomax (topiramate).   **Available in:** 25, 100, 200 mg tablets; 15, 25 mg sprinkle capsules. **Comments:** Another newer anticonvulsant being used for childhood psychiatric problems; likely a third- or fourth-choice medication.

Lithium Carbonate

Although there are several brands of lithium available, their preparations are similar, with the same available doses, side effects, and considerations. These brands are grouped together here as "lithium salts."

Preparations

Lithium salts (Lithobid slow-release capsules, Eskalith capsules and Eskalith ER tablets).   **Available in:** 150, 300, 450 mg tablets or capsules; 1 tsp suspension (equivalent to 300 mg tablet). **Prescribed for:** Best-known treatment for very irritable, angry, and aggressive behavior of children diagnosed with bipolar disorder. **Dosing information:** Smallest dose available (150 mg) is given twice a day and increased weekly until behavior symptoms have improved or side effects occur; ultimate dosage may reach as high as 1800 mg a day. Checking blood levels of lithium after 5 days of treatment at prescribed dose can be helpful, primarily to check compliance and/or risks of side effects. **Side effects:** Nausea; vomiting; stomach pain; tremor (shaking hands); sedation; increased urination and liquid intake; higher risk of dehydration during routine "stomach flu"; acne eruptions common; kidney and thyroid function must also be monitored. **Comments:** Lithium was considered highly effective for the control and prevention of bipolar disorder symptoms when the diagnosis (then called manic-depression) was a more restricted and discrete set of symptoms. This is a difficult drug to take and is rarely used in preteens; many teens find it too unpleasant to continue to use, even when it is helpful.

Tricyclics

Prescribed for: Sometimes used for anxiety, agitation, and depression; now rarely used for impulsivity, inattention, and hyperactivity. **Side effects:** Sedation, dry mouth, blurred vision, constipation are common. **Dosing information:** Usually, lowest dose available is given to start and increased every four to five days; doses beyond double the usual adult starting dose are controversial because of risk of rare catastrophic events (see comments). **Comments:** Tricyclics were widely prescribed for children in the 1990s until several sudden deaths, presumably caused by irregular heart rhythms (arrythmias), were reported; electrocardiograms (EKGs) recommended before beginning a tricyclic and after achieving a steady dosage. Currently there is little reason to use these medications in children unless alternative classes of medications have failed.

Preparations

Imipramine (Tofranil).   **Available in:** 10, 25, 50, 75, 100, 150 mg tablets. **Dosing information:** Usual starting dose is 10 or 25 mg. **Comments:** Best known of the tricylics for pediatric use. Low doses still occasionally used to treat bedwetting (but conditioning machines or the drug desmopressin, also known as DDAVP, are treatments of choice for nocturnal eneuresis).

Desipramine (Norpramin).   **Available in:** 10, 25, 50 75, 100, 150 mg tablets. **Comments:** Least sedating of tricyclics, once widely used to treat stimulant-resistant ADHD.

Nortriptyline (Pamelor and Vivactyl).   **Available in:** 10, 25, 50 mg capsules; 10 mg/tsp suspension.

Elavil (amitriptyline).   **Available in:** 10, 25, 50, 75, 100, 150 mg tablets. **Comments:** Elavil is the most sedating of tricyclics; may still be used in low doses for relief of pain (e.g., for headache).

Anafranil (clomipramine).   **Available in:** 25, 50, 100 mg tablets. **Comments:** Used widely for a brief time in the 1990s for OCD symptoms, but replaced by SSRIs because of its sedating effects.

Antihypertensives

Preparations

Clonidine (Catapres).   **Available in:** 0.1, 0.2, 0.3 mg scored tablets; 1, 2, 3 skin patch delivery system (worn on hairless region of body and delivers the daily mg requirement of oral doses). **Prescribed for:** Initially tested for control of high blood pressure in adults but now used for control of impulsivity, inattention, distractibility, irritability, and insomnia (usually due to a stimulant); also used as a first treatment for control of Tourette's syndrome. **Dosing information:** Lowest dosage is given at first, usually not more than twice a day (even though blood levels of drug show medication lasting only 3 to 4 hours); dose is increased weekly until improvement in behavior or side effects occurs; skin patch is changed weekly. **Side effects:** Sedation; dizziness upon rising; possible "rebound" hypertensive crisis if drug is stopped abruptly (very rare at dosage levels prescribed for childhood psychiatric problems). **Comments:** Clonidine is rarely used alone for ADHD symptoms but often used in combination with a stimulant; often used in late afternoons or evenings to treat "rebound" effect of stimulants or when stimulants cause insomnia. Combination of clonidine and stimulant has been ambiguously associated with several reports of sudden death attributed to cardiac heart beat irregularities (arrythmias), so electrocardiograms before and while taking this combination are recommended. Clonidine is less sedating and probably less effective for the treatment of Tourette's than Haldol.

Tenex (guanfacine).　　**Available in:** 1, 2 mg tablets. **Comments:** A longer-lasting drug with actions similar to clonidine, requiring only once-a-day dosing.

Atypical Antidepressants

This category is a loose grouping of several drugs that were initially released for the treatment of adult depression but have since—like many other psychiatric medications—been used for a variety of adult and childhood problems.

Preparations

Wellbutrin (bupropion).　　**Prescribed for:** Second choice for inattention and impulsivity; might be tried as first choice for teens or adults where potential stimulant abuse is of concern; also for depressed mood and/or possibly for agitation. **Available in:** 75, 100 mg tablets; 100, 150 mg sustained-release (SR) tablets. **Side effects:** Generally well-tolerated, some irritability at high doses, risk of seizures at very high doses. **Dosing information:** Most doctors are choosing SR option for twice-daily dosing, starting with lowest dose once or twice a day; typical adult total daily dose is 300 mg. **Comments:** Wellbutrin is not as effective as the stimulants for ADHD symptoms nor as effective as the SSRIs for improved resiliency or mood. Could be second choice for either set of symptoms, or first choice when combined symptoms are present.

Effexor (venlafaxine).　　**Prescribed for:** Primarily mood elevation; possibly also for agitation. **Available in:** 25, 37.5, 50, 75 mg scored tablets; 37.5, 75, 150 mg extended-release (XR) capsules. **Side effects:** Similar to tricyclics—modest sedation, dry mouth, etc.; theoretical risk of cardiac arrythmias in children. **Dosing information:** For tablets, lowest dose is usually given twice or three times daily, increasing every week to two weeks; XR given once a day in either A.M. or P.M.; typical adult dose is 150 mg daily total. **Comments:** Effexor is promoted as having broader effects than SSRIs on neurotransmitters. However, effects are very similar to the older tricyclics, which were once dismissed as producing more side effects than the SSRIs. Effexor may have a place as second- or third-choice medication.

Trazodone (Desyrel).   **Prescribed for:** Initially promoted as mood elevator but found to be too sedating; now used in low doses to promote sleep, often when another psychiatric drug, such as a stimulant or SSRI, is causing insomnia. **Available in:** 50, 100, 150, 300 mg tablets. **Side effects:** Can cause priapism, a very painful, persistent penile erection.

Serzone (nefazodone).   **Available in:** 50, 100, 150, 200, 250 mg tablets. **Side effects:** Too new to thoroughly evaluate manufacturer's claims of fewer side effects than older tricyclics. **Comments:** Newer antidepressant; might be used as a third- or fourth-choice medication.

Remeron (mirtazapine).   **Available in:** 15 mg tablets. **Side effects:** See Effexor. **Comments:** Very new antidepressant; might be used as a third- or fourth-choice medication.

Antianxiety Drugs

Prescribed for: Relief of anxiety, fears, panic episodes, and for inducing and maintaining sleep. **Side effects:** Sedation (may be desired); possible severe respiratory depression or death when combined with alcohol; except with Buspar, possible long-term development of tolerance (the need for more and higher doses) and addiction (craving and withdrawal). **Dosing information:** In general, the lowest available dose is tried first and increased until sedation occurs; the only major differences among these drugs are how quickly they take effect and their length of action (described below for individual preparations); medications with rapid onset of action are generally desirable as hypnotic (sleep-inducing) agents; agents with longer duration of action are preferred for daytime control of anxiety. **Comments:** These drugs tend to be less effective in children than in adults, as daytime sedation occurs at doses that control fears or anxieties; continued use for either anxiety or insomnia is discouraged because of tolerance/addiction risk; occasionally children become agitated (disinhibited) instead of sedated on low and moderate doses.

Preparations

Xanax (alprazolam).   **Available in:** 0.25, 0.5, 1, 2 mg scored tablets. **Dosing information:** Relatively rapid onset (30 minutes); moderate length of action (4 to 6 hours). **Comments:** Widely prescribed for daytime control of anxiety.

Ativan (lorazepam).   **Available in:** 0.5, 1, 2 mg tablets. **Dosing information:** See Xanax. **Comments:** Widely prescribed as a midrange antianxiety agent.

Halcion (triazolam).   **Available in:** 0.125 0.25 mg scored tablet. **Dosing information:** See Xanax. **Comments:** Concerns over mental confusion with use in the elderly have somewhat decreased its use.

Valium (diazepam).   **Available in:** 2, 5, 10 mg scored tablets. **Dosing information:** Slightly slower onset of action than Xanax but overall is very similar. **Comments:** Venerable, best-known "doll" of the 1950s, carries adverse publicity of tolerance and addiction; however, these risks exist for all drugs of this class except Buspar.

Klonopin (clonazepam).   **Available in:** 0.5 mg scored tablet; 1, 2 mg tablets. **Dosing information:** Slower onset of action (60 minutes) with longer duration of action (6 to 8 hours). **Comments:** Current choice for full-day coverage of anxiety.

Ambien (zolpidem).   **Available in:** 5, 10 mg tablets. **Dosing information:** Rapid onset of action (20 minutes), with short duration of action promoted as ideal for sleep induction without leaving a next-morning "hangover." **Comments:** Somewhat different chemical structure than other sleep-inducing agents, but not especially different from Xanax and much more expensive.

Sonata (zaleplon).   **Available in:** 5, 10 mg capsules. **Dosing information:** See Ambien. **Comments:** See Ambien.

Buspar (buspirone).   **Available in:** 5, 10, 15 mg tablets. **Dosing information:** Moderate onset of action lasting for 6 to 8 hours; can be taken two or three times a day. **Comments:** Different structure and action than other antianxiety agents; appears to cause less sedation and no tolerance or addiction; appears less effective overall than other antianxiety agents in this class but could be used fairly safely for mild anxiety problems.

INDEX

ABOUT THE AUTHOR

Lawrence H. Diller, M.D., practices behavioral-developmental pediatrics and family therapy in Walnut Creek, California. He lives nearby with his wife and two teenage sons. He is the author of *Running on Ritalin: A Physician Reflects on Children, Society, and Performance in a Pill* (1998). He won the Society for Professional Journalism's 2000 Award for Public Affairs for "Kids on Drugs" in Salon.com. In May 2000 he testified as an expert for a congressional subcommittee investigating Ritalin use in America.